Breaking the Mold of Education

Innovative and Successful Practices for Student Engagement, Empowerment, and Motivation

Audrey Cohan and Andrea Honigsfeld

ROWMAN & LITTLEFIELD EDUCATION
A division of
ROWMAN & LITTLEFIELD PUBLISHERS, INC.
Lanham • New York • Toronto • Plymouth, UK

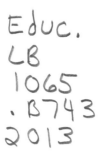
Published by Rowman & Littlefield Education
A division of Rowman & Littlefield Publishers, Inc.
A wholly owned subsidary of The Rowman & Littlefield Publishing Group, Inc.
4501 Forbes Boulevard, Suite 200, Lanham, Maryland 20706
www.rowman.com

10 Thornbury Road, Plymouth PL6 7PP, United Kingdom

British Library Cataloguing in Publication Information Available

Library of Congress Cataloging-in-Publication Data

Andrea Honigsfeld and Audrey Cohan
Breaking the Mold of Education : Innovative and Successful Practices for Student Engagement, Empowerment, and Motivation / edited by Andrea Honigsfeld and Audrey Cohan.
p. cm.
Includes bibliographical references.
ISBN 978-1-4758-0350-1 (cloth : alk. paper) -- ISBN 978-1-4758-0351-8 (pbk. : alk. paper) -- ISBN 978-1-4758-0352-5 (electronic)
1. Linguistic minorities--Education. 2. Children of minorities--Education. 3. Multicultural education. 4. Language and culture. I. Honigsfeld, Andrea, 1965- II. Cohan, Audrey.
LC3731.B655 2012
371.829--dc23

2011050653

Printed in the United States of America

We dedicate this book to educators who made teaching their career. We continue to be inspired by all the preservice and inservice teachers, teacher educators, and school and district administrators who have ever shared their powerful stories of perseverance, innovation, and change.
Thank you!

A very special personal acknowledgement goes to Eileen and Norman Feinsilver; Barry, Jeffrey, Lauren and Matthew Cohan; as well as Howard, Benjamin, Jacob, and Noah Honigsfeld.
Your love and support keep us going!

Contents

Acknowledgments

We would like to extend our gratitude to the authors who generously contributed a chapter to this volume and shared their stories of innovation. We would also like to thank our friends and colleagues at Molloy College, Rockville Centre, New York and beyond, who have supported us through multiple research and publication projects, celebrated the release of the previous three *Breaking the Mold* volumes, and encouraged us to complete the series.

A special thank you to our research assistants Marcella Amenta, Katherine Lapelosa and Taylor Volpe, whose meticulous attention to detail while working on this final volume is greatly appreciated.

This project would not have been possible without the support of Dr. Tom Koerner and the hard-working staff of Rowman and Littlefield Publishing. Thank you!

Foreword

Kenneth C. Williams

The illiterate of the 21st century will not be those who cannot read and write, but those who cannot learn, unlearn, and relearn.—Alvin Toffler

Each book in the *Breaking the Mold* series offers visionary insight and cutting-edge information about the field and practice of education. This edition, which focuses on overall student engagement, targets a subject that has been of paramount importance to me throughout my career. As a teacher, an assistant principal, principal, and now speaker and consultant, I have dedicated myself to advocating for high levels of learning for all students. As such, paradigm shifting and mold breaking have become second nature to me.

After reading the *Breaking the Mold* series and speaking with Audrey Cohan and Andrea Honigsfeld, I knew that I had found like-minded individuals. I was thrilled to be invited to write the foreword for this latest volume, and after reading each contribution, my excitement only grew. Each of these authors is challenging the reader to aspire to higher levels of literacy by both learning and unlearning. Collectively, they are asking readers to challenge mindless precedents that consistently prove antiquated or just plain faulty, and, in the absence of those precedents, they are speaking of empowerment, best practice, shape-shifting action, professional reflection and collaboration, and high expectancy for all learners.

This volume of the *Breaking the Mold* series both validated and challenged many of my long held beliefs and practices. It is not just another book on the topic of student engagement. Instead, this text offers its readers the opportunity to become passionate practitioners, continuous learners, and strategic cage rattlers!

To provide some context for the content of this book, I would like to begin with some simple yet very relevant facts. First, the nature of the global workforce has been changing and will continue to change rapidly. Where we once had a labor force that relied heavily on industrial and simple managerial jobs, we now have one that relies on skills like self-guidance, communication (often with people who are in different countries or from different cultures), information application, and problem solving.

Bernie Trilling and Charles Fadel, who are board members at the Partnership for 21st Century Skills, made the point that the shift into what many are now calling the "Knowledge Age" will be as significant as was the shift from "the Agrarian Age into the Industrial Age" (as cited in Marzano & Heflebower, 2012, p. 4). This means that in order to be successful, our students need to be able to do more than simply memorize facts—they need to be adaptable. They need to be able to both learn and unlearn quickly to keep pace with today's workforce. It stands to reason that only the most engaged students will be able to process information quickly, synthesize it, determine which information is relevant for a given task, and disregard irrelevant information. However, our students are not engaged.

A recent National Education Association survey revealed that, according to teachers, 60 percent of all students are generally "disengaged" or "unmotivated" (Golde, 2011). If 60 percent of our students are not engaged enough to keep up with the demands of today's workforce, we will clearly face dire consequences as a society.

But why are our students not engaged? Is this trend dramatically different than past generations? To understand the answers to these questions, we have only to look at the world around us. Technology has advanced with dizzying speed in the 21st century; students are inundated with infinitely more information competing for their attention virtually all of their waking hours. Any parent of a teenager has seen his or her child working on a school assignment while downloading files, chatting with friends online, and listening to music or talking on the phone.

With massive changes such as these, is it any wonder that the same instructional techniques used to engage students in earlier centuries simply aren't working anymore? Clearly, the world is changing, and in order to help our students keep up with it, our educators must become more adaptable as well; they must unlearn antiquated instructional techniques and learn new, more effective ways to engage today's learners.

Along with all of the new opportunities and interests competing for the attention of our students, we also have to consider what science now tells us about their attention spans (Marzano, Pickering, & Heflebower, 2010):

- For pre-adolescents: Change-up in instruction is necessary approximately every 5–10 minutes.
- For adolescents into adults: Change-up in instruction is necessary approximately every 10–20 minutes.

With new data like this, teachers cannot afford to simply expect students to sit still and pay attention during lectures. We know now that students have limits, and in order to engage them, educators must work within their boundaries. They must, once again, unlearn old ways and learn new, more effective instructional techniques.

With a bit of context on the discussion of student engagement, I can now say that what impresses me about the contributions that Cohan and Honigsfeld have skillfully selected and assembled is that, together, they have shifted the essential question:

- From: Why aren't students more engaged?
- To: How can we make our classrooms more engaging?

The previous discussion makes the clear point that we already understand why our students are not engaged. More than a decade into the 21st century, it is time to stop asking why engagement is so low and start asking what we as educators are going to do about it.

From beginning to end, *Breaking the Mold of Education: Innovative and Successful Practices for Student Engagement, Empowerment, and Motivation for the 21st Century* is addressing this question. Each of these contributions offers research, new (and sometimes provocative) perspectives, and problem solving techniques that empower the reader to both learn and unlearn, and do what is necessary to connect with today's learners.

Della R. Leavitt and Erin N. Washington's chapter, "I Teach Like You Are All Gifted: Leading Lowest Track Students to Become Confident Mathematics Learners" speaks to a critically important intangible. That intangible is the power of teachers' self-efficacy. While I am an ardent opponent to tracking as a grouping practice, I acknowledge that the practice still exists. That said, it is one thing to lead a class of students in the lowest track and expect them be successful, it is another thing to teach the students as if they were all *gifted.*

I worked to establish a culture of high expectations from day one. I found this idea both inspiring and validating, as teaching with this mindset has been a longtime practice of mine. As a classroom teacher, I took this approach every year. I'd tell my students that they were hand selected for my class; I would tell them that they were gifted and would be taught accordingly. I emphasized that our classroom had both "soft floors and high ceilings," and that I had high expectations for each of them.

The level of efficacy that the authors highlight in this chapter has as its goal to increase and deepen the efficacy of the students for whom they serve. This idea is supported by books such as *The Highly Engaged Classroom* by Marzano et al. (2010).

In that text, Marzano and his colleagues identify four questions that teachers must support students in answering affirmatively with regard to student engagement. The last of those questions is, "Can I do this?" This last question is all about what teachers can do to deepen the level of efficacy in students. The teacher highlighted by Leavitt and Washington demonstrates practices that have an impact on the struggling learners highlighted in the piece and can impact all learners across the learning spectrum.

Lastly, Wendy LaRue and Peter Hoffman-Kipp's chapter, "Montessori High Schools: Where Long-Standing Tradition Meets the Cutting Edge*"* really hit home for me. As an educator and a parent, I have firsthand experiences to offer on this issue, and this chapter just strengthened my resolve. On the one hand, I am a life-long supporter of public education. I am a career educator; I've been a teacher, an assistant principal, principal, and now an author and consultant. I've spent my career seeking out and executing best practices to ensure learning for all.

On the other hand, I'm also the proud parent of a son who has a learning style that just does not jive well in the traditional school environment—an environment often steeped in rigid routine and inflexibility. We found that a factory-model structure was not going to get the best out of our son. Adam was drowning in the traditional school environment. By all accounts and measures, he is a more than capable student. Moreover, he does well on the state standardized assessments. However, after an exasperating two years of struggling, we decided to try a Montessori high school.

While there was an adjustment period during which he had to both learn and unlearn things, he has definitely turned a corner. The authors highlight several findings that represent absolute bull's-eye reasons for his success. Their findings suggest that:

> (a) the integrated curriculum, which encourages students to make connections in their learning, (b) the freedom students are afforded in the classroom, (c) the caring relationships that are forged between students and teachers, and (d) the experiential approach to learning work in tandem to relate the education experiences to the students' roles in society, thus meeting their developmental needs. (LaRue & Hoffman-Kipp)

This chapter asks important questions: What about a typical high school transcript reflects anything about which student is invested and passionate? What can we take from the Montessori model that will help us make learning more relevant and authentic for all students? The authors make a strong case that if students were generally engaged in more personalized learning, they might feel more connected to their learning, to their community, and to humanity because they would be supported in developing a deeper understanding of the web of life. If students were provided plentiful opportunities to increase their self-worth through authentic work via service learning and internships, they would be better prepared to be good stewards of themselves, other people, and the environment.

In short, each of the contributors to this volume has put forth solid, thought-provoking ideas that, if fully embraced by a dedicated audience, will no doubt play a part in making the critical changes necessary in contemporary education. After thoroughly reading and digesting the content, I am confident readers of this volume will be better and more reflective educators. As such, it is my great honor to introduce *Breaking the Mold of Education: Innovative and Successful Practices for Student Engagement, Empowerment, and Motivation for the 21st Century.*

REFERENCES

Golde, S. (2011). *The future of computer technology in Coolidge Unified School District.* Retrieved from http://tinyurl.com/ctauvkl

Marzano, R. J., & Heflebower, T. (2012). *Teaching and assessing 21st century skills.* Bloomington, IN: Solution Tree Press.

Marzano, R. J., Pickering, D. J., & Heflebower, T. (2010). *The highly engaged classroom.* Bloomington, IN: Solution Tree Press.

Preface

From the beginning of our work on innovation, we have wanted to contribute to the professional literature a book about what we called the "E's" of learning: student eagerness, empowerment, engagement, enthusiasm, excellence, and energy. We anticipated that the journey of editing the *Breaking the Mold* series would lead us to answer an essential question about what *really* empowers students to become academically successful. Students have always been at the core of our inquiry. And yet, once we arrived—as it is the case with many explorers—there was no simple answer.

As we began our quest to find out how to best empower students, we had several core beliefs that undergirded our thinking. We recognized that there is no single program or idea that can close the expanding achievement gap among groups of students as it currently exists either culturally, socioeconomically, academically, or strategically. But we did believe that there was compelling evidence of grassroots successes around the country and around the world that must be shared and celebrated.

It has been our passion and our goal to cull these documentary accounts for educators who are dedicated to empowering their students—may they be struggling, marginalized, or awaiting challenge. To this end, we hope that our readers will note the creativity in each of these stories and find inspiration within them. We also believe that collaboration is at the root of each successful program and the research has certainly supported this notion (Cohan, Honigsfeld, & Mordowitz, 2012; Honigsfeld & Dove, 2012).

Each narrative in this volume is built upon collaboration and ongoing dialogue among stakeholders; be it teachers, teachers and students, students and students, community members, or any other constituencies. In addition, we found that behind almost all successful innovations there was a driving force of a visionary change agent with powerful leadership skills.

In our professional conversations and interactions with colleagues, we had discussed the value of concise accounts as a vehicle for sharing new initiatives, groundbreaking ideas, and positive, well-documented practices. What we knew was that teachers and administrators often learn by sharing real-life examples and knowing that authentic, innovative ideas have been successfully implemented with actual students. They resist when told what could be, or should be, or might be successful. Instead, they see the benefits of meaningful innovations for *breaking the mold* in different realms of education.

At no other point in history, we believe, education, *the art and science of teaching, and teaching effectiveness* (Marzano, 2007) have been so misunderstood and criticized. We believe the language of education has to be a positive one; students must feel supported and parents should appreciate the quality education that is attainable. We hope to showcase creative, unique, and constructive ways that educators have strived to meet their students where they are and then raise hopes, expectations, and performance.

Similar to our previous three volumes, *Breaking the Mold of School Instruction and Organization: Innovative and Successful Practices for the 21st Century* (Honigsfeld & Cohan, 2010), *Breaking the Mold of Preservice and Inservice Teacher Education: Innovative and Successful Practices for the 21st Century* (Cohan & Honigsfeld, 2011), and, *Breaking the Mold of Education for Culturally and Linguistically Diverse Students: Innovative and Successful Practices for the 21st Century* (Honigsfeld & Cohan, 2012), the purpose of this book is to offer a carefully selected collection of documented best practices for empowering students.

The contributing authors represent diverse backgrounds, cultures, and experiences, yet their chapters recognize similarities among students so that the innovations can be transferred to other contexts. As with the previous volumes, we have invited well-established authors to share their practical, research-based success stories as well as have included authentic accomplishments documented by first-time authors.

The 20 chapters in this volume are organized into four sections: (a) making personal connections and engaging students in reflection; (b) engagement with literacy and language; (c) music, movement, arts, drama and other creative engagements; and (d) school culture, community, and student success. We are hopeful that the compelling chapters shared in this volume—focused on innovation and transformation—will help thrust education and teacher action (rather than reaction) in a positive trajectory of change.

REFERENCES

Cohan, A., & Honigsfeld, A. (Eds.), (2011). *Breaking the mold of preservice and inservice teacher education: Innovative and successful practices for the 21st century.* Lanham, MD: Rowman and Littlefield.

Cohan, A., Honigsfeld, A., & Mordowitz, S. (2012, April). *Towards a new model of educational innovations: 90 ways to define research-based initiatives.* Paper presented at the AERA Convention, Vancouver, Canada.

Honigsfeld, A., & Cohan, A. (Eds.), (2010). *Breaking the mold of school instruction and organization: Innovative and successful practices for the 21st century.* Lanham, MD: Rowman and Littlefield.

Honigsfeld, A., & Cohan, A. (Eds.), (2012). *Breaking the mold for culturally and linguistically diverse students: Innovative and successful practices for the 21st century.* Lanham, MD: Rowman and Littlefield.

Honigsfeld, A., & Dove, M. (Eds.), (2012). *Coteaching and other collaborative practices in the EFL/ESL classroom: Rationale, research, reflections, and recommendations.* Charlotte, NC: Information Age Publishing.

Marzano, R. J. (2007). *The art and science of teaching: A comprehensive framework for effective instruction.* Alexandria, VA: ASCD.

I

Making Personal Connections and Engaging Students in Reflection

> We cannot expect children to become excited about learning if we are not
> excited about teaching and learning. That is a simple fact. Let's change the
> way we interact with our students. Let's excite them. Let's inspire them be-
> yond their imaginations. (Peters, 2007, p. 98)

This section of the book focuses on the connections made between students
and their teachers, the use of reflective practice, and examples of inspiration-
al teaching as pathways to enhance student achievement.

Yolanda Sealey-Ruiz recognizes the challenge of making the school a
safe setting to engage in conversation and serious inquiry about race and
cultural differences. She asks, "If schools aren't such a place, where else will
these conversations occur?" She notes that even as we acknowledge that race
and diversity need to be included in the curriculum, such curriculum is virtually absent. She suggests ways to activate students' racial literacy and to
recognize how the urban youth culture contributes to education.

Shannon T. Page, Andrew P. Charland, April A. Scott, and Hiller A.
Spires share their passion for project-based inquiry as a way to embrace
emerging technologies and create an innovative school setting with multiage
grouping. Through their documentary account, they describe a dynamic context for learning as technology tools are used to engage student interest,
which in turn, can be created in other school settings.

Next, Angela K. Salmon and Thomas G. Reio Jr. consider ways to nurture
student curiosity by fostering teachers' purposeful self-evaluation skills and

enhancing teachers' reflective practice. Through the implementation of the *Visible Thinking* approach, a culture of thinking is developed and ultimately improves instructional practice.

Finally, Nancye E. McCrary, Susan N. Wood, Kate Larken, and Sioux Finney document the Civic Engagement Project, which targets the knowledge, skills, dispositions, and social action essentials for a pluralist and participatory democracy. This unique collaboration produced a scalable curriculum that targets three areas—civic engagement, persuasive writing, and media design and production—and involves university members, teachers, administrators, and the larger community.

Within this section, many authors support the contention that schools should embrace learning environments that encourage open-ended curiosity, exploration, imagination, creativity, and reflection, as well as student responsibility for identifying and solving problems. The challenge, for educators and policy makers, is to clearly examine the concepts of motivation, reflective practice, positive school environments, as well as to consider ways to listen to the voices and experiences of students in support of their successful academic and social development.

REFERENCE

Peters, S. (2007). Capture, inspire, teach! Reflections on high expectations for every learner. In A. M. Blankenstein, R. W. Cole, & P. D. Houston (Eds.), *Engaging every learner* (pp. 83–99). Thousand Oaks, CA: Corwin Press.

Chapter One

Using Urban Youth Culture to Activate the Racial Literacy of Black and Latino Male High School Students

Yolanda Sealey-Ruiz

Teachers, I realize that there is a pink elephant in almost every educational setting that we refuse to acknowledge… and that is race. That word seems to bring out virulent feelings in people.—Gerald, 12th grade

For the past decade my work in and out of the classroom has allowed me to do one of the things I love most—get people to talk about race. My work as a research associate at New York University required that I mobilize school districts to investigate the disproportionate representation of the Black and Latino boys in special education in their K–12 schools. Their disproportionality required the districts' teachers and administrators to examine their policies, practices, and beliefs about this population of young people in their schools. It also required deep and often uncomfortable discussions about race, racism, stereotypes, inequality, inequity, and white privilege.

At the start of each professional development project, most school personnel, particularly teachers, cringed at the thought of engaging in these conversations across ethnic, racial, cultural, and linguistic lines. Over the months and years of our work together, the conversations gradually became easier to facilitate, but not necessarily easier for them to have; these conversations require "safe spaces" and unbridled humility and vulnerability—positions of discomfort. Perrone (1991) reminds us why discussions about race are so difficult but important to have:

We have struggled in schools to engage issues of race and cultural differences constructively, but we haven't yet learned how to speak about such matters, embedded as they are with guilt, shame, confusion, superiority, and inferiority. Even as we tend to acknowledge that race and issues of difference need to be central to the curriculum, that curriculum is virtually absent. Our challenge is to make the school a safe setting to engage in conversation and serious inquiry about race and cultural difference. If schools aren't such a place, where else will these conversations occur constructively? (p. 48)

Because I continue to teach high school while teaching at the college level, I have the privilege of engaging both students and preservice teachers in conversations about race, oftentimes bringing the two groups together to learn from each other.

EMBRACING DIFFERENT WAYS TO TALK ABOUT RACE

The purpose of this chapter is to briefly describe Urban Youth Culture (UYC) as it appears in the literature and as I have witnessed it in my high school classroom of all Black and Latino male students.[1] It also seeks to encourage educators to realize that these conversations are not as difficult to have if we welcome their various forms of expression. For example, critique of school and society may not always flow as naturally for students within a five-paragraph essay or even during a discussion in a *safe space*.

I have learned that some of my students best describe their feelings and express their opinions and beliefs, particularly about sensitive issues like race and racism, through spoken word, haiku, rap lyrics, artistic, or digital renderings. My students who connect with their Urban Youth Culture quite naturally engage in *racial literacy*—a skill that consists of deep and critical discussion on the issues of race, racism, and societal inequities. These conversations are rarely welcomed in classrooms, in part because of the time limits placed on instruction as a result of the hyperstandardized testing climate in public schools; and teachers feeling the strain of the ethnic, racial, cultural and linguistic differences that exist between them and their students.

Furthermore, educators often do not view students' artistic abilities as skills, but as elements of a culture that compete with the goals of school. Educators must bridge these differences. One way to do this is to embrace the positive aspects of Urban Youth Culture and realize that critical conversations about race and racism promote a student's critical thinking, as well as self and societal examination. When students connect to their Urban Youth Culture and activate their racial literacy, this helps to build their understanding of how systems of oppression work in American society.

STUDENT ENGAGEMENT IN URBAN YOUTH CULTURE (UYC)

Urban Youth Culture (UYC) is used as a generic term for hip-hop culture, which over the last 37 years, has evolved from creative urban expressions such as rapping, dj-ing, break dancing (b-boying and b-girling), and graffiti art to a cultural movement that encompasses music, graffiti art, dance, poetry, and fashion, and also promotes Black and urban consciousness.

Often UYC is at the center of societal controversy and debate. At one end of the spectrum the very nature of UYC is criticized, and censorship is suggested. At the other end of the spectrum, UYC is characterized as perpetuating the status quo and enhancing corporate and American hegemony (White, 2004). Little is said of the positive and innovative elements of youth culture in general, which makes it difficult to find public commentary on UYC that does not seek to disparage or censor the voices of urban youth.

In the early 1970s, hip-hop was born as a product of social action in the Bronx River Projects of the South Bronx. Afrika Bambaataa (Bambaataa Kahim Aasim), a former "War Lord" of the street gang, the Spades, and leader of the Zulu Nation organization is the father of hip-hop consciousness.

In an effort to end the gang violence that plagued the South Bronx at the time, Bambaataa, along with the technical genius of DJ Kool Herc, organized large block parties where young people came to channel the tensions of the street through dancing and socializing in a safe and positive environment (Chang, 2005). Rap, as an art form, began as personal narrative, telling the individual stories of urban lives ignored by the mainstream media. By the mid-eighties, hip-hop took the main stage both as a cultural phenomenon and as a commercial success.

Throughout the 1980s and 1990s, hip-hop solidified itself as a culture that involved the aforementioned forms of artistic urban expression (rapping, dj-ing, breakdancing and graffiti art) while utilizing the Black power and civil rights movement traditions of community uplift and empowerment. Hip-hop's participation in the larger (American) culture provides a vehicle for urban youth, and urban Black and Latino youth in particular, to resist the status quo of disempowerment that has been prescribed for them. Greeson (2009) in fact, defined hip-hop culture as

> an outgrowth of the Civil Rights and Black Power Movements, the hip-hop movement represents the African American youth initiative to define itself and construct an urban pedagogy, a way of understanding and renegotiating how life in these urban communities could and should be lived. As a culture, hip-hop deals with music, language, dress style, and politics. (p. 151)

Early on, Rose (1994) argued that ''Hip Hop is a cultural form that attempts to negotiate the experiences of marginalization, brutality, truncated opportunity, and oppression with the cultural imperatives of African American and Caribbean history, identity and community'' (p. 21). Large numbers of Black and Latino urban youth connect with hip-hop culture. It influences their understanding about life, politics, and everyday choices.

Over the past three decades, globalization and de-industrialization have continued to eliminate jobs, foster higher levels of inequality, and further marginalize low-income urban communities. Urban youth have been particularly impacted by this transformation. The continued failure of urban school districts to provide equitable educational outcomes comparable to middle-class and wealthier school districts, the lack of jobs available for lower skilled workers, insufficient health services, and an increase in the disproportionate placement of urban youth of color in special education and discipline programs have placed large numbers of low-income urban youth at risk.

These young people are aware of their position in society, even if they are not sure what action to take to improve it. Urban Youth Culture provides a platform to critique their situation and sometimes dream new possibilities for themselves and those in their communities.

PROMOTING RACIAL LITERACY

At Teachers College, I conceived and executed (with the assistance of three English Education Master's students)[2] a forum called *Racial Literacy Roundtables*. Racial Literacy Roundtables (RLRs) are informal discussions, which seek to foster open dialogue about race and issues pertaining to race so that such dialogue can make its way into our classrooms and research more explicitly.

With funds from my college's Diversity and Provost offices, I recruit Master's and doctoral students, and scholars from various universities to facilitate two-hour conversations around the topics of race and racism for the Teachers College community. Past participants have included my high school students, Teachers College and Columbia University students, alumni, and faculty. The RLR facilitators have the freedom to choose their topic and often engage multimodal literacies (the use of photos, music, art, or film, etc.) to ignite the discussion.

During our RLR sessions, over refreshments, participants delve into their understanding of race and some of their experience with racism in their daily lives. The RLR series and my work with public school districts against disproportionality have offered the opportunity to engage thousands of (mostly) adults in discourse on race. Many describe our conversations as "liberating," "eye-opening," and "essential," yet the majority of these educators are nervous about welcoming their students into these discussions.

Activating students' racial literacy allows them to develop critical analysis skills and to examine America's institutionalized racist structures; they come to understand that their current situation is influenced by forces beyond their control. Then, they must be given space to discuss how with this knowledge they can devise appropriate strategies for their academic and social success. These discussions are relatively easy for them *and* for me because the environment in my classroom is one where all of their literacies—cultural, racial, and distinctly urban—are welcomed, and in fact, are required rules for engagement.

REMIX: ACTIVATING RACIAL LITERACY THROUGH URBAN YOUTH CULTURE

For the Black and Latino young men in my high school classroom, hip-hop culture is a way of life. This is reflected in their media consumption—the books they read, the music they listen to, the movies they watch and the video games they play. Their Urban Youth Culture provides a lens for them to view themselves and the world around them, including the universe of school.

I noticed over the past year that whenever my high school students critiqued the social construction of race in American society and talked about racism's impact on their lives, they frequently referenced the lyrics of rap songs written and performed by international and American–based hip-hop artists to help illustrate their points and support their arguments.

In my classroom, there were explicit connections made between race and their lived experiences. For example, the students were given an assignment for which they had to construct a written response to the following prompt: "What would you say if you had the opportunity to speak from your heart to your teachers about issues of race in school? Please start your response with "Dear Teacher(s)":

Although they inferred that a written response was expected, I was prepared for my students to construct their responses using multimodal literacies (Haddix & Sealey-Ruiz, 2012). I expected that they might compose their responses using smart phones, i-movie, PowerPoint, or take pen and pencil to their journals or sketchbooks. In response to this assignment, Jared wrote and performed a rap to the beat of a popular song at the time:

My School Bluz
by Jared[3] a.k.a. "Dr. Smoove"

You say I got potential, you bring the credentials,
Ultimately you hold the key to learning E-ssentials
I'm in school—Ready! But all I get is jokes

Kids prankin, & cursin, clogging up the bano with smoke.
Dear Teacher: You say you care—
but your actions don't match
You say 'you down for me' but all I feel is trapped
Testing, standardized madness, craziness, messiness
That don't make sense!
Who drivin' this bus again?
Cuz we about to crash on our ass & at the
speed we goin this mad dash gonna start some blood flowin'
I'm in school so teach me & my brother
Can't you see us for potential and not for our color?

Gerald, a college-bound senior, who is quoted at the beginning of this chapter, wrote an essay accompanied by an i-movie that included photos of family members and of himself from kindergarten through the 12th grade. All of Gerald's photos were taken in and around the schools he attended. The flow of the slideshow was set to snippets of "99 Problems" by Jay-Z (2003), and "Black Codes" by Wynton Marsalis (1990). Gerald wrote,

Dear Teacher,
I need you to understand that you having low expectations of me would never propel me to greatness, because no one rises to low expectations. Remember feeling sorry for us, will never allow us to grow. Meet us where we are as scholars and stop stereotyping, which continues to stagnate and contaminate.

Most students come with a level of racial literacy, but this skill is not valued in schools, in part, I believe, because it does not appear on a standardized test and is not embraced by most educators. To create an environment conducive to discussions about race and racism, I spent a considerable amount of time and energy during the first few weeks of school building a cohesive and open classroom community.

In addition to using culturally responsive literature and articles which related to their home lives and popular cultures, students completed activities that asked them to talk about their childhood, their neighborhood, tell their name story, and write their racial autobiography of school. Students were asked to deeply think about their experiences with race, and be both reflective and reflexive (about their attitudes and beliefs).

They read texts that were meant to complicate their understanding of race and racism and equip them with language to talk about these two concepts. They activated their Urban Youth Culture without prompting, and willingly engaged in conversations explaining why they chose one mode of communication over another. Rap, a feature of Urban Youth Culture, rooted in a tradition of protest, was a popular and natural mode of expression for many of my students to respond to the notion of race and the effects of racism.

CONCLUDING THOUGHTS

The voices of urban youth, and particularly Black and Latino males, are marginalized or muted in our society and in our classrooms. These students are not often provided outlets to discuss the toll that racism takes on their daily lives. Despite the fact that many Americans desire it, we are not living in a postracial society.

Racism is still a problem that impacts the quality of life of everyday people, especially young people of color who are often disempowered in schools, and disenfranchised in society—from being too young to vote to having adults not take them seriously for their opinions and beliefs. In a progressive educational environment, Urban Youth Culture can provide a platform for the racial literacy of young people to flourish. This creates the possibility for young people—and young Black and Latino males in particular—to have their voices heard and skills respected.

REFERENCES

Chang, J. (2005). *Can't stop, won't stop: A history of the hip-hop generation.* New York, NY: St. Martins Press.

Greeson, A. D. (2009). *Race and education.* New York, NY: Peter Lang Primer Series.

Haddix, M., & Sealey-Ruiz, Y. (2012). Cultivating digital and popular literacies as empowering and emancipatory acts among urban youth. *Journal of Adolescent and Adult Literacy, 56*(3), 189-192. doi: 10.1002/jaal.00126

Jay-Z. (2003). 99 Problems [Jay-Z]. On *The Black Album* [Audio Compact Disc]. New York, NY: Roc-A-Fella Records.

Marsalis, W. (1990). Black Codes. [Wynton Marsalis]. On *Black Codes* [Audio compact disc]. NY: Sony.

Perrone, V. (1991). *A letter to teachers: Reflections on schooling and the art of teaching.* San Francisco, CA: Jossey-Bass.

Rose, T. (1994). *Black noise: Rap music and Black culture in contemporary America.* Hanover, NH: University Press of New England.

White, C. (2004, January). "Morally panicked:" Engaging youth culture for social efficacy in schools. *Online Journal of Urban Youth Culture, 2*(1). Retrieved from http://juyc.info/archived/volumes/panicked.html

NOTES

1. My students are members of an all-male, in-school mentoring group (UMOJA) founded by Mr. Erik Nolan. This is a specially designed class that enrolls only the students of UMOJA. They receive high school credit for this class.

2. Emily Carman, James Kang, and Lauren Gengo, all of whom are now full-time teachers who engage their students in racial literacy practices, were Master's students at Teachers College, Columbia University in 2009 when the Roundtables were formed.

3. Pseudonym.

Chapter Two

Embracing Project-Based Learning with Emerging Technologies in the Multiage Classroom

Shannon T. Page, Andrew P. Charland, April A. Scott, and Hiller A. Spires

The purpose of this chapter is to describe an innovative, multiage classroom (4th and 5th grades combined) that uses project-based learning as its primary pedagogical approach. Additionally, technology tools are used to engage student interest and enhance critical thinking skills. The first two authors teach the multiage class at A. B. Combs Elementary Leadership Magnet School in Raleigh, North Carolina; the other two authors, who teach project-based learning in teacher education courses at North Carolina State University in Raleigh, also collaborate with the A.B. Combs's teachers.

WHY USE MULTIAGE GROUPING AND PROJECT-BASED LEARNING?

Coupling multiage grouping with project-based learning can provide a dynamic context for learning that meets learners where they are, as Hoffman (2003) explained: "In multiage classrooms, teachers structure learning activities to meet individual student needs rather than aiming toward the middle of the class" (p. 1). Flexible grouping strategies can facilitate teacher-led guided practice of key skills in small group settings in addition to student-led groups in which students collaboratively investigate shared topics of interest.

Daniel (2007) reported that although research findings about the benefits of multiage grouping on achievement are inconclusive, there is considerable evidence that multiage grouping promotes "enhanced student self-esteem,

11

decreased behavioral referrals, formation of close communities, and social and academic continuity" (p. 3). Multiage structures provide students the opportunity to develop different dynamics for learning in which they can create relationships that foster a sense of responsibility and caring with other students who are at different developmental levels in the class.

Project-based learning, which builds on a strong orientation to real-world problems, is an effective instructional approach that can readily incorporate new technologies and media (Buck Institute for Education, 2009). The content generated from the learning activities can be enhanced with Internet resources enabling a wide range of digital texts, allowing learners to share the results of their work with extended and distant audiences while gathering feedback and potential inspiration from others' work. Research indicates that in some cases project-based learning has proven effective with long-term retention as well as skill development and satisfaction of students and teachers (Strobel & van Barneveld, 2009).

As educators, we see the need for school learning to mirror the world around us and to embrace the possibilities that the future holds for students. We are faced with industrial age education policies that are outdated and do not focus on developing the whole child for the 21st century. In the current knowledge age, it is important for students to take in vast amounts of information from many resources and be able to filter through the information while working with peers in collaborative situations.

The 21st century skill set involves a blending of the content of the three R's (reading, writing and mathematics) with the four C's (creativity and innovation, communication, collaboration, and critical thinking and problem solving) (Trilling & Fadel, 2009). The teacher's role is to be a facilitator and coach as the learner makes content connections and constructs new meanings. In order to engage students in a successful project-based learning process, the teacher needs to (a) hold high expectations for all students to succeed, (b) value inquiry and intellectual curiosity, and (c) embrace global learning and cultural diversity. The multiage classroom coupled with project-based learning provides a dynamic context to galvanize student learning for the 21st century.

PROJECT-BASED LEARNING: THINK BIG, START SMALL

We encourage teachers who are just beginning a project-based learning process to think big but start small. To guide the project we used five phases: (a) asking a compelling question, (b) gathering and analyzing information, (c) creatively synthesizing information, (d) critically evaluating and revising, and (e) publishing, sharing and acting (see Figure 2.1).

These phases provided an instructional sequence for students to move through the inquiry and creation process. They also provided opportunities for teachers to explicitly facilitate informational mini-lessons that scaffolded students' skills in creating their final product, which in this example was a Google site demonstrating what they had learned. The project took place over a three-week time frame. During class, we provided mini-lessons as needed that aligned with the five-phase process; students worked in small groups of 3–4 both in and out of class to finalize their projects (see Figure 2.1).

In addition to the five-phase process that kept students on track, below we discuss five areas that teachers should keep in mind as they conduct project-

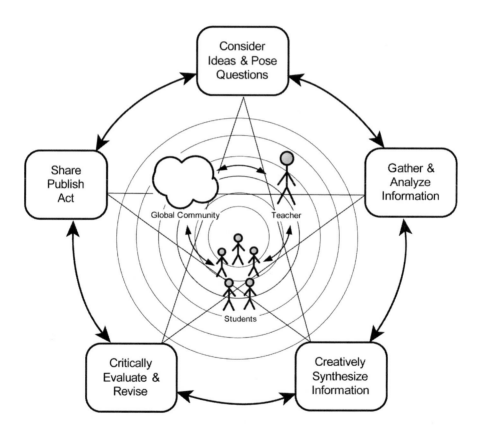

Figure 2.1. **The Five Phases of Project-Based Learning**

Used with permission. Spires, H., Wiebe, E., Young, C., Hollebrands, K., & Lee, J. (2009). *Toward a new learning ecology: Teaching and learning in 1:1 learning environments.* **Friday Institute White Paper Series. NC State University: Raleigh, NC.**

based learning: (a) gauging student interest, (b) establishing goals and outcomes, (c) designing formative and summative assessments, (d) gathering information, and (e) integrating technologies to support student learning.

Gauging Student Interest

The key to successful project-based learning is to create a student-centered learning environment. Research on well designed learning projects geared to students' interests and passions have demonstrated that internal motivation can contribute to active engagement, deeper understanding, and a desire to learn more (Darling-Hammond, 2010). When teachers gauge interest first, learners are able to dive deeper into their projects because of their personal connections with the content. This stimulates the brain and causes students to become more curious; in turn, curiosity drives questions, which allows learning to be sustained over time.

In order to assess student interest we used surveys that also identified learning styles. Students created bubble maps with topics they wanted to learn about, they combined their bubble maps with 5–6 peers, and then we typed all of their topics into a Wordle (www.wordle.net). This gave the class and teachers a visual to see the topics about which the majority of the class was interested. As teachers, we consistently kept our eyes and ears open to find new topics that the students were curious about, since student focus is dynamic and may change throughout the year.

An example of a specific topic that we studied this year was ancient Greece and Greek mythology. Students had opportunities to become interested in mythology thanks to children's chapter books such as *The Lightning Thief* (2005) and *The Red Pyramid* (2010) both by Rick Riordan. When we asked students to list topics they wanted to learn more about, we immediately saw ancient Greece and Egypt as the top categories. Students voted to determine if our next project would focus on ancient Greece or ancient Egypt. After ancient Greece won, we began the brainstorming process to build our learner-centered curriculum.

Establishing Goals and Outcomes for the Project

As we planned for the project, we constantly referenced the Rigor and Relevance Framework developed by the International Center for Leadership in Education (www.leadered.com). We decided that students would create a website to show their understanding of ancient Greece, participating in collaborative teams with 4th and 5th graders combined. The teams worked on their website together making sure that everyone took ownership of his or her own learning as well as the learning of others.

We created a virtual field trip, in which the students planned and budgeted the class trip to Greece in order to learn about ancient Greece and mythology. Key to our success as teachers was the capacity to modify our plans quickly, since we could not be sure of the exact path that the project would take. We needed to be flexible since we could not predict the ways in which students might process information or the questions they might ask. Our goals and outcomes included:

1. Teach the district and state content standards while keeping the students engaged in a dynamic learning experience;
2. Design projects that use technologies and a collaborative process, which would prepare students to be adept at 21st century skills;
3. Engage student interest and curiosity to drive the project; and
4. Demonstrate what students learn through a combination of formative and summative assessments.

Designing Formative and Summative Assessments

A variety of authentic assessments are vital to maintain student engagement, as well as rigor, during the project-based learning process (Spires, Hervey, Morris, & Stelpflug, 2012). It is important to be clear about the relationship between performance-based assessments associated with project-based learning and standardized tests that are required by the district and state. We used a combination of formative and summative assessment approaches that included the following:

1. Quick-writes at the end of mini-lessons in order for students to demonstrate their content learning. This provided us with important information so that we could design appropriate mini-lessons to support student learning.
2. Small group discussions to check for understanding. If students misunderstood concepts, we would reteach the ideas or engage in peer teaching.
3. Teachers, peers, and parents assessed final projects based on predetermined elements of a rubric (e.g., overall design of the website, accuracy of content, appropriate references for content, and quality of collaboration). Feedback on the same criteria from different constituencies provided rich and diverse feedback on the projects.
4. The content and process of the project were aligned with standardized assessments (e.g., North Carolina End of Grade Test) so that students, administrators, and parents could see how the project content supported the district's and state's testing program.

Gathering Information

In order to be effective with project-based learning, it was important to plan ahead by gathering key resources to support the students' inquiry and learning process. We did this by collecting student-friendly websites about Greece.

After finding resources related to district and state standards, we used the Curriculum Integration Wheel (www.leadered.com) to make sure the alignment was in place. To ensure that we were covering the necessary objectives, we analyzed our 4th and 5th grade curricula to determine which objectives we could cover while studying Greece. We identified objectives in social studies, science, math, and language arts. We knew that creating a budget for accommodations, travel expenses, food, and sightseeing would cover many of our math objectives. For our science objectives we were able to focus on landforms. There were many websites that allowed students to view landforms that are located throughout Greece along with information about the formation of specific landforms. These were explicit ways in which we used student interest first to guide our project and then determined how to match the learning outcomes to our state standards.

Integrating Technologies to Support Student Learning

We must equip students with the skills necessary for life in the 21st century, as well as help children navigate when and how to use the proper technological tools and resources. As part of our project-based learning activity, we conducted mini-lessons on how to strategically search for information on the Web and evaluate its accuracy and relevancy.

Lessons involved direct modeling of the use of Boolean search techniques, differentiating between domain names (.com versus .org), and querying sites for accuracy and transparency. During project-based learning, we used the following tools to support student engagement and learning:

1. iPod Touches and iPads—The students used iPod Touches and iPads in order to research information about their chosen topics. The students were able to record notes on the notepad application. Students also used the voice recorder in order to keep track of ideas that they wanted to include on their website.
2. Computers—The students used laptops and desktops to research and create their Google Site. They also used Microsoft Word in order to type the information that they wanted to include on their website. Typing the information in Word allowed them to use spell-check for spelling accuracy and formation of sentences.

3. Google Site—The students worked in groups of 3–4 to research cho-sen topics about Greece and then created a Google Site to organize, synthesize, and share their information.
4. Video Conferences—Our class was able to Skype with students in Greece in order to discuss the Grecian way of life, landscape, and famous historical sites such as the Parthenon. The video conference experience made the information come alive!
5. Flip Cameras for Video Creation—The students utilized flip cameras to record conversations and group work in order to assess how well they were collaborating. Having students watch the recording of them-selves as they collaborated was engaging as well as instructive. This also allowed the teachers to monitor group work to make sure groups were staying on task and collaborating in fruitful ways.

CHALLENGES AND EVIDENCE OF SUCCESS

As educators, we found it initially difficult to create support throughout our school and community for multiage and project-based learning. It took time for us to research and inform others about the benefits of both multiage classrooms and project-based learning, since both of these approaches were new to our school. Another challenge that we faced was the mismatch be-tween the way that we teach and how the district and state assess our stu-dents.

Using project-based learning gave our students opportunities to become creative problem-solvers and critical thinkers. The process encouraged them to dig deep into relevant content topics while forming their own opinions. Unfortunately, district and state assessments do not require students to think deeply about ideas or topics but rather test factual information that may or may not be of interest to the learner. The third challenge that we faced was the lack of technology tools initially needed for the project (i.e., iPod Touches, iPads, and laptops).

We asked parents to allow students to bring one of these tools from home if they were available. In some cases, parents purchased new tools and donat-ed them to the class. Combined with the tools that we already had at the school, we eventually had enough technology to make the project successful since students were collaborating in teams. We allowed students to take turns taking the technology home so they could do research outside of class as well.

There are several ways that we know our approach with multiage and project-based learning was successful:

1. The students were visibly engaged with the learning process. Students came to class each day eager to get started with their work; many of the students did extra work at home in order to move their projects along during class. We were motivated by how frequently students expressed how much they enjoyed creating their projects, working collaboratively, and using technology. There was a clear difference in levels of student engagement with this project versus other learning approaches we have used.

2. We received positive feedback from parents at our Celebrate Success Day. At the end of the unit, parents attended class to view student project results. The students were successful in involving parents in an active learning process during the event, which proved particularly powerful. Students demonstrated their knowledge about ancient Greece and mythology as well as their facility with technology in ways that was informative for parents. In exit interviews, 100 percent of the parents expressed that they learned new information during the event and were pleased and often surprised by the depth of knowledge about ancient Greece, mythology, and technology tools that the students had acquired. One parent commented, "I was surprised at how comfortable the students were with the content they had learned, with the technology they were using to demonstrate their projects, and with collaborating with each other to share projects. They functioned as a team."

3. The content and process we used met the objectives and standards outlined in the North Carolina Standard Course of Study. Students demonstrated proficiency with the content through their portfolio artifacts, including the websites they generated on ancient Greece and mythology. The portfolios showcased ongoing research, with teacher and peer feedback based on key rubric elements tied to the state standards. The next time we conduct the project, we will use outside experts to evaluate the student portfolio of work. We believe that students will respond positively to external feedback, producing an even higher quality of work.

CONCLUSION

We have a vision of schools in which all students are so excited about learning that they can hardly wait to arrive each morning. We have a vision of schools with few discipline problems because students are focused on engaging content that leads to the creation of innovative projects supported by the latest technology. We have a vision of schools in which all students master the four basic language skills (reading, writing, speaking, listening) and math as a regular part of participating in dynamic projects. We believe that multiage grouping and project-based inquiry, along with innovative uses of emerging technologies, hold promise for creating a visionary learning culture in schools.

REFERENCES

Buck Institute for Education. (2009). *PBL starter kit: To-the-point advice, tools and tips for your first project*. Retrieved from http://www.bie.org/tools/toolkit/starter

Daniel, L. (2007). *Research summary: Multiage grouping*. Retrieved from http://www.nmsa.org/Research/ResearchSummaries/MultiageGrouping/tabid/1282/Default.aspx

Darling-Hammond, L. (2010). *The flat world and education: How America's commitment to equity will determine our future*: New York, NY: Teachers College Press.

Hoffman, J. (2003). Multiage teachers' beliefs and practices. *Journal of Research in Childhood Education, 18*(1), 5–17.

Riordan, R. (2005). *The lightning thief*. New York, NY: Hyperion Books.

Riordan, R. (2010). *The red pyramid*. New York, NY: Hyperion Books.

Spires, H., Hervey, L., Morris, G., & Stelpflug, C. (2012). Energizing project-based inquiry: Students, read, write, and create videos. *Journal of Adolescent and Adult Literacy, 55*, 483–493.

Spires, H., Wiebe, E., Young, C., Hollebrands, K., & Lee, J. (2009). *Toward a new learning ecology: Teaching and learning in 1:1 learning environments*. Friday Institute White Paper Series. NC State University: Raleigh, NC. Retrieved from http://fi.ncsu.edu/podcast/white-paper-series/2009/04/22/toward-a-new-learning-ecology/

Strobel, J., & van Barneveld, A. (2009). When is PBL more effective? A meta-synthesis of meta-analyses comparing PBL to conventional classrooms. *Interdisciplinary Journal of Problem-based Learning, 3*(1). Retrieved from http://docs.lib.purdue.edu/ijpbl/vol3/iss1/4/

Trilling, B., & Fadel, C. (2009). *21st century skills: Learning for life in our times*. San Francisco, CA: John Wiley & Sons.

Chapter Three

Nurturing Curiosity by Teachers' Purposeful Self-Evaluation and Reflective Practice

Angela K. Salmon and Thomas G. Reio Jr.

The art of teaching demands creative solutions based on the teaching and learning goals that teachers set in their practice. For over six years, senior teachers at the Biltmore School in southern Florida and the lead author employed action research to find ways to engage children's thinking by nurturing their curiosity and making their thinking visible. This effort allowed both teachers and children to build upon their demonstrated curiosity and thinking to improve learning (Salmon, 2010a).

For Ana, the lead teacher, Johanna the toddler teacher, and Sindy, the kindergarten teacher, being able to engage the students in productive thinking or in understanding concepts had been an arduous journey considering that children are naturally curious, but they are not yet sophisticated, polished thinkers. Thus, unless the conditions for curiosity and learning are appropriate, the child will avoid thinking beyond the minimum requirements of solving a problem (Willingham, 2009).

Ana, for instance, was interested in having her first grade students understand how Martin Luther King Jr. and the Civil Rights movement influenced evolving laws dealing with human rights. Using the See/Think/Wonder thinking routine (Ritchhart, Church, & Morrison, 2011) to examine photographs that discriminated Black people from White people, she presented students with pictures of two lavatories. The first one was an old rusty one for Black people and the other was a new white one for White people. After scrutinizing the picture and sharing observations among themselves, the children made interpretations of what they saw that generated dialogical thinking (Paul, 2001).

Consequently, when a child shares his or her observations or interpretations with a peer, it often stimulates the other children's curiosity to focus on things not previously noticed and to generate new questions to explore the situation in greater breadth and depth (Reio, Petrosko, Wiswell, & Thongsukmag, 2006). In our example, by looking at these images, the children empathetically came up with the question "Why didn't people like each other?" This inquiry engaged them in conversations that later guided them to future investigation.

CREATING CULTURES OF THINKING

In an effort to accomplish their goal of fostering optimal student learning, the teachers at the Biltmore School had been committed to creating cultures of thinking in the classroom by implementing the Visible Thinking Approach (Ritchhart et al., 2011) to enhance their teaching.

Visible Thinking is an approach to teaching and learning that emphasizes the use of thinking routines and documentation to make thinking more visible in classrooms. Thinking routines—being research-based and well tested by scholars and teachers—are relatively easy-to-follow, step-by-step strategies that support both the development of students as self-directed learners and learning for understanding (Ritchhart & Perkins, 2008; Ritchhart et al., 2011).

The teachers found the use of documentation a powerful means to capture the students' thinking and support the improvement of their teaching. To help document their practice, the teachers used video-documentary techniques and pictures and took notes as well. The action research engaged the teachers in a systematic collaborative reflection on the documentation they shared (Salmon, 2010b). In the group reflections, the teachers became aware of the nature of their classroom discourse and how it affected students' responses.

Each time the teachers visited and revisited the documentation and reflected upon it with their peers, they refined their understandings of the tone that they were setting in their classrooms and how this tone influenced students' learning. These group reflections also stimulated their own curiosity to expand the breadth and depth of investigative activities related to achieving their teaching goals.

One of the major challenges encountered by the teachers was sparking the children's curiosity, as they discovered the need to ask the appropriate kinds of questions or risk not engaging the students. For example, in observing Johanna, a toddler teacher reading (and asking questions about) a book about caterpillars, colleagues noted that her questions were initially too narrow and thus the children's engagement with the teacher and thinking suffered; however, when she used thinking routines that used open-ended questions, there was a noticeable difference.

See Table 3.1 for the two types of interactions that follow as they either stimulate limited teacher–child interaction and thinking (narrow questions) or more engaged interaction and thinking (open-ended questions).

WHY CURIOSITY AND THINKING?

A dramatic technological revolution is guiding the new millennium. This condition challenges the educational goals for the 21st century. Increasingly, employers and societies in general are looking for graduates who are eminently curious, successful problem solvers, comfortable working with ambiguity, and creative (Reio et al., 2006).

Among the skills for adapting successfully in the 21st century, curiosity and imagination are among the most important motivational elements that promote learning and subsequent adaptation (Reio et al., 2006). Thus, schools should consider learning environments that encourage open-ended curiosity and exploration with "no right answer," creativity, and taking personal responsibility for identifying and solving problems.

Narrow Questions	Open-Ended Questions
Teacher reading a book about caterpillars (before individual and group reflection upon observing a video-documentary)	Teacher reading a book about spiders (after individual and group reflection upon observing a video-documentary)
Teacher: A bee has what?	Teacher: What's going on here? (showing picture)
Child: Legs.	Child: The spider doesn't want to go play.
Teacher: Is the caterpillar happy or sad?	Teacher: What makes you say that?
Child: Sad.	Child: She doesn't want to play because his legs are making a web.
Teacher: What is the caterpillar doing?	
Child: Flying.	

Table 3.1

Examples of Teacher–Child Interactions Guided by Narrow Questions versus Open-ended Questions

Curiosity, the desire for new information and sensory experiences (Reio et al., 2006), is an intrinsic learning motivator that invites children to be open to learning, unlearning and relearning, exploring, and developing problem finding skills.

Thinking routines are structures that engage children in thinking and being curious. Ritchhart et al. (2011) presented several thinking routines such as:

- See/Think/Wonder (What do you see? What do you think? What are you wondering?)
- Connect /Extend/Challenge (Make connections to what you know about a topic. How does the topic extend your thinking? What challenges do you have?)
- Explain/Provide Evidence (What makes you say that?)

Among other things, implementing these thinking routines creates a classroom climate where inquiry and the quest for understanding are embraced for the sake of optimal learning. The thinking routines thus operate as tools that scaffold and promote higher order thinking.

Educators should highlight the importance of determining what is worth learning in their classrooms and how to educate best for dealing effectively with the unknown because they are educating students in preparation for the ambiguous contingencies that arise in day-to-day life (Perkins, 2009). Indeed, when students are in a classroom where they feel safe risking to inquire, it allows them to view things from their own perspective, which stimulates their curiosity, creativity, imagination, and discovery—all vital elements of teaching for the unknown (Reio, 2010).

THE POWER OF GOOD DOCUMENTATION

Rinaldi defined documentation as a tool for recalling; that is, it is a possibility for reflection (as cited in Project Zero & Reggio Children, 2001). For Rinaldi, the education path becomes visible through in-depth documentation of the data related to classroom activities, making use of verbal, graphic, and video-documentary techniques.

Teaching is an art that requires the teacher to adeptly listen, observe, and assess his or her practice for the sake of creatively designing novel, provoking learning environments that stimulate and sustain the student's curiosity. Observation and documentation shape, extend, and make visible children's and adults' individual and group learning. Observation and documentation then becomes an integral part of the procedures aimed at fostering learning and for productively modifying the learning–teaching relationship (Project Zero & Reggio Children, 2001).

Because learning is a social and cultural process driven by the learners' curiosity (Reio, 2010), as the teacher observes the students' interests, abilities, and theories about the world, he or she can identify ways to create zones of proximal development and suitably scaffold children's learning (Vygotsky, 1978). In their journey, the teachers at the Biltmore School learned how to listen to the children and become strategically selective in what they needed to document for further analysis and reflection. By consulting among themselves about what transpired during their observations, teachers were increasingly able to make sense of the data acquired from their documentation efforts.

With easy access to current technology, the teachers frequently used video-documentary techniques to share their experiences in the classroom with their learning community. The learning community tended to be a risk-free environment that engaged the teachers as learners and provided useful information that helped them make educated pedagogical decisions (Reio, 2010).

By participating in the community, the teachers risked being vulnerable in front of their colleagues to acquire new information, experiment with new ideas, and construct new knowledge about how best to handle their classroom practice. In the aforementioned example of the interaction between the toddler teacher and children, she was videotaped reading the book to the children.

Later, in a study-group session with her learning community, the teacher's colleagues focused their attention on the communication patterns, including the type of questions she used while reading to the children. After it became clear that the teacher's narrow questioning may have been unnecessarily limiting, there was a distinct change in the teacher's discourse while reading a second book. On this second occasion, she used open-ended questions that valued children's prior knowledge and fostered their curiosity to know more.

NURTURING CURIOSITY THROUGH THINKING ROUTINES

The interplay between nature and nurture is a condition that determines how adults inhibit or enhance children's learning. Unlike more traditional approaches to learning that focus on mastery of content at the expense of nurturing inquiring attitudes, teachers should work to create and develop students' thinking dispositions (Perkins, 2009; Ritchhart, 2002; Salmon, 2010b).

These thinking dispositions guide students' decisions in day-to-day life as expert problem solvers, thoughtful decision makers, and creative thinkers. Children are such curious individuals, with a natural disposition to explore, question, and wonder about the world, and teachers are responsible for cultivating this inquiring habit of mind in them (Reio et al., 2006). Teachers as facilitators are responsible for nurturing habits of mind through appropriate modeling, guided discovery, and scaffolded learning experiences.

Teachers' discourse in the classroom is a critical condition to create a culture of thinking and curiosity. Upon revisiting her documentation, Sindy found it useful to record the questions she commonly used and analyzed the range of children's responses. At this point, she classified the yes/no or narrow responses from the children as well as questions that generated other questions.

Sindy believed the thinking routines facilitated her job in engaging children in thinking with evidence and provoking curiosity in the kindergarten children while developing a deeper understanding of concepts. For example, while studying about countries by using the 3-2-1 Bridge—a routine which consist of 3 words, 2 questions, and 1 metaphor to activate prior knowledge before a learning experience begins—the children began to make connections between the countries being examined, their own country, and world issues.

Sindy was surprised with the connections that the children began making with the new information and their demonstrated level of understanding. Accordingly, when a student presented her research about Italy, the other children began to make analogies such as, "Pasta is the main dish for Italy," just as "Tacos are for Mexico."

When students talked about the Roman Coliseum, one noted that the Coliseum was a place for war, as people do not know how to solve their problems with words these days. This is a good example supporting the notion that "… by asking questions, selecting terms, clarifying ideas and processes, providing data, and withholding value judgments, we can stimulate and enhance the thinking of others" (Costa, 2008, p. 194).

As the children were engaged in these conversations, they became aware of the language of thinking that allowed them to learn how to learn. The children were very familiar with terms such as *analogy, cause and effect, hypothesis,* and so forth, to explain how they process the information necessary to understand a concept. For Sindy, the meta-cognitive process helped her students become more aware of the things that they wanted to explore; in other words, the potential of understanding these types of thinking processes fostered children's curiosity.

While analyzing the different types of family structures around the world and their eating habits, for instance, the children in Sindy's classroom made hypotheses as to where these families came from in terms of habitats, activities, economy, and traditions. This example demonstrates how dialogical thinking can stimulate children's curiosity to a higher level.

IMPLICATIONS

The thinking routines are goal oriented, allowing Sindy to introduce the children to the cognitive term "analogy." Costa (2008) noted that the use of specific cognitive terminology evokes thinking in others by causing children to examine their own thinking and enhance their self-concept as thinkers.

Teaching and learning is a dynamic exchange of thoughts, questions, and actions between students and teachers. Thus, it is beneficial for both teachers and students to examine their own work and reflect upon it. By sharing experiences through documentation, teachers have the opportunity to grow as individual and group learners (Salmon, 2010b). It is necessary though to have a structure that allows teachers to use lenses that help them become more focused on what they are seeking. This focusing action could be done by articulating the teaching and learning goals with the guiding questions for observations.

With these few examples, we were able to share the value of teachers as listeners who tried improving their practice through purposeful self-evaluation and reflective practices. The teachers found it useful documenting their classroom discourse with special emphasis on the questions they were asking the students. Although the teachers found it challenging to craft questions that promoted higher order thinking and at the same time nurture curiosity in the children, they were acutely aware that this was a critical aspect of expert teaching practice. Thus, the thinking routines were a practical aid to accomplishing their goal.

CURIOSITY AS AN INNOVATION THROUGH THE VISIBLE THINKING APPROACH

If curiosity is natural in human beings, then why is it that some students do not like school? If teachers support Willingham's (2009) notion that children do not like school because the mind is not designed for thinking, then it is critical for teachers to design learning experiences that engage students in thinking by provoking curiosity, inquiry, and understanding. The Visible Thinking approach facilitated the development of a culture of thinking that built upon both teacher and student curiosity.

Teacher curiosity led to documenting instruction, consultation with peers, and reflection that was used to implement the Visible Thinking approach and ultimately improve instructional practice. Student curiosity generated by the teachers' improved practice supported not only finding creative solutions to problems, but most importantly, creating a habit of question and problem posing to increase the possibility for a sense of wonderment and further curiosity.

NOTE

All names used in this chapter are pseudonyms.

REFERENCES

Costa, A. (2008). *The school as a home for the mind: Creating a mindful curriculum, instruction and dialogue.* Thousand Oaks, CA: Corwin Press.

Paul, R. (2001). Dialogic and dialectical thinking. In A. Costa (Ed.), *Developing minds: A resource book for teaching thinking* (pp. 427-436). Alexandria: VA: Association for Supervision and Curriculum Development.

Perkins, D. (2009). *Making learning whole: How seven principles of teaching can transform education.* San Francisco, CA: Jossey-Bass.

Project Zero & Reggio Children (2001). *Making learning visible: Children as individual and group learners.* Reggio Emilia, Italy: Reggio Children.

Reio, T. G., Jr. (2010). What about adolescent curiosity and risk taking? In J. L. DeVitis & L. Irwin-DeVitis (Eds.), *Adolescent education: A reader* (pp. 99–109). New York, NY: Peter Lang.

Reio, T. G., Jr., Petrosko, J. M., Wiswell, A. K., & Thongsukmag, J. (2006). The measurement and conceptualization of curiosity. *The Journal of Genetic Psychology, 167,* 117–135.

Ritchhart, R. (2002). *Intellectual character: What it is, why it matters, and how to get it.* San Francisco, CA: Jossey-Bass.

Ritchhart, R., Church, M., & Morrison, K. (2011). *Making thinking visible: How to promote engagement, understanding and independence for all learners.* San Francisco, CA: Jossey-Bass.

Ritchhart, R., & Perkins, D. N. (2008). Making thinking visible. *Educational Leadership, 65*(5), 57–61.

Salmon, A. (2010a). Making thinking visible through action research. *Early Childhood Education Journal, 39*(1), 15–21.

Salmon, A. (2010b). Engaging children in thinking routines? *Childhood Education, 6,* 132–137.

Vygotksy, L. (1978). *Mind in society.* Cambridge, MA: Harvard University Press.

Willingham, D. T. (2009). *Why don't students like school?* San Francisco, CA: Jossey-Bass.

Chapter Four

Partnerships for the Common Good: Democratic Citizenship Through Writing, New Media, and the Arts

Nancye E. McCrary, Susan N. Wood, Kate Larken, and Sioux Finney

What does it take to develop and maintain a democracy? What models of teaching and learning inspire students to participate? What partnerships foster innovation? Currently, a three-year implementation study, the Civic Engagement Project, designed at the University of Kentucky targets knowledge, skills, dispositions, and social action essential for a pluralist and participatory democracy.

By the end of its pilot year, the Civic Engagement Project had enabled a unique collaboration that produced a scalable curriculum targeting three areas: civic engagement, persuasive writing, and media design and production. Eighth-grade students, such as Adrian featured in this chapter, demonstrated growth in all areas.

As an example of the process, Adrian, an eighth-grade student at Woodford Middle School (Woodford County, Kentucky), was uncertain what to research. "At first, all I knew was I wanted to paint something," she said, "and then I read the history of Simmons Elementary. It was started as a segregated school for Black students. In 1954 after the court ruling, six students from Simmons chose to attend the White high school, and the next year Simmons became a school for everyone."

Adrian was inspired by this account and decided to study the history of racism in her rural Kentucky county. "After gathering my information and doing the research," she explained, "I imagined the lives of two girls, one Black and one White, during the integration of Woodford Public Schools in the 50s, and I produced a visual art piece with Black and White hair styles that eventually end up 'woven together.'" Her original abstract painting was exhibited in the public library (see Figure 4.1).

As a primary goal of social studies, educators in the United States have developed numerous approaches to teaching and learning about democratic citizenship. Few, however, have fully integrated writing, civics, and the arts in ways that *personalize* democratic action. For example, Project Citizen, a national civic education organization, often provides curriculum materials that focus on the mechanics of democratic government (i.e., how legislation is passed or how branches of government operate).

The Civic Engagement Project, on the other hand, uses inquiry-based approaches, blending didactic information with creative modes of representation that engage learners in refining and making public *their own voices* to inspire community action (see Figure 4.2).

A PEDAGOGICAL APPROACH TO CIVIC ENGAGEMENT

The Civic Engagement Project was implemented in three classrooms: rural, suburban, and urban, with eighth-grade students identified as unlikely to

Figure 4.1. Adrian Teegarden, *Untitled*, 2011 (32 X 36 in, Acrylic on canvas).

Photographer: Susan Nelson Wood

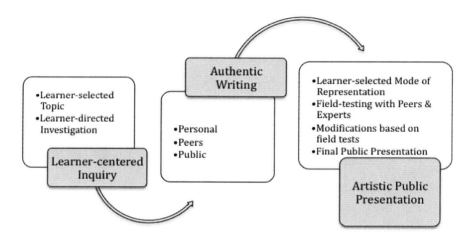

Figure 4.2. Civic Engagement Curriculum Model

become active participants in democratic life (Parker, 2006). The four-phase project invited adolescents to utilize action-research methods to address real-world critical issues in their home/local communities and then work with a range of partners to represent their findings publically.

Inquiry learning aimed at civic engagement involves productive thinking that extends the application of knowledge, skills, and dispositions rather than reproductive thinking that may promote problem solving in similar situations but does not transfer to novel instances or events (McCrary & Mazur, 2010). Engaging students in real-world community-based problems situates learning in contexts that personalize social action and mediate the development of knowledge and skills that promote self-efficacy, which is likely to extend beyond adolescence to adulthood. Such generative learning can have a long-term impact for the common good of local communities.

Civic Dispositions and Civic Engagement

Students direct the communitywide empowerment project. In collaboration with their teachers, they enact a service-learning curriculum employing action research methods to address real-world critical issues in their home/local communities. Table 4.1 identifies some of the topics addressed during the pilot project. For example, eighth graders in urban Fort Thomas, Kentucky, started by researching the local history surrounding the Underground Railroad. Increasingly, they found themselves interested in other instances of subversive activity in their community, such as the history of organized crime in the area, and so began an investigation into issues related to local authority.

As a measure of change as a result of the Civic Engagement Project, we used civic dispositions identified by the Kentucky Department of Education in pretest and posttest questionnaires. The 13 dispositions included: (a) patriotism, (b) open-mindedness, (c) negotiation and compromise, (d) civility, (e) compassion, (f) critical mindedness, (g) persistence, (h) respect for the rights of others, (i) respect for the law, (j) honesty, (k) ambiguity, (l) civic mindedness, and (m) courage.

Students ranked each disposition on a scale from 0–4, with 0 indicating they did not understand the disposition and 4 indicating they understood and acted on the disposition. Additionally students wrote brief reasons for their scores. From initial (pretest) scores in the 0–1 range, students who participated in the project were more likely to shift scores to 3–4, generally. More important, students were asked to note dispositions they would like to strengthen, which created a conscious awareness about dispositions they deemed more or less desirable.

Many students struggled with *ambiguity*, defined in the pre- and posttests as "willingness to accept that some things will not be clear to me the first time and that there is not always one right answer to every question." Jeffery said, "I like to know *right* and *wrong*," and added a goal for improvement to be willing to accept the lack of clarity of situations, questions, and ideas.

Learner-selected Topics	Modes of Representation
Teen dating abuse	Website
Racial segregation in Woodford County, KY	Original abstract painting
The life of the first person to live in our historic home	Digital documentary
War veterans of our community	Powerpoint presentation
L. L. Pinkerton	Prezi online presentation
Governors from Woodford County, KY	Moviemaker and YouTube videos
Air pollution in Oldham County, KY	Video
Discrimination	Public service announcement—Call to action
Animal homelessness	Twitter page, Photo-story, and YouTube video
Child abuse	Video
Animal cruelty	Storykit on iPad
Natural disaster response and relief	Website
Illegal immigration	Facebook page
Homelessness	Facebook page and poster
Healthcare for veterans	Public service announcement
Violence and bullying	Video/audio slideshow with Splice
Comparing our lives with those of child soldiers	Video
Affirmative action	Storybook

Table 4.1

Sample Inquiry Topics Selected by 8th-Grade Students in the Civic Engagement Project

Another said, "I know there isn't an answer for everything [but] I like to have an answer for things."

Students also struggled with *courage*. Austin said: "I sometimes lack the courage to stand for what I believe in because I am afraid of what people will say." He added that he would like to "speak up in large groups more often." Similarly, Jordan ranked himself at a 2 on courage because "even though I have strong beliefs, I have trouble speaking out about them." Clearly, these students valued *courage* and wanted to be more willing to take a stand publically, yet most were initially afraid to do so. Generally they scored themselves higher on *courage* in post-tests and tied their knowledge gains to greater willingness to speak publicly.

Persuasive Writing

Rather than write for purposes most often associated with a traditional instructional model—assigned by a teacher for a grade—students in the Civic Engagement Project wrote for a variety of purposes and audiences. According to pre- and post-intervention samples of their writing, students developed new skills as writers.

Three practical and principled innovations of how writing is taught in the Civic Engagement Project served as a scaffold, a kind of logical progression, in helping students think more deeply about audience, abstraction, and media. This progression includes refinement as students first write for themselves, then they write for peers, and finally they refine their writing for larger, unknown audiences, such as listeners or viewers of radio and television programs, public service announcements, or public performances.

The inquiry process was developed as a sequence and a spiral curriculum to be implemented over the course of a year. The writing curriculum is highly collaborative and based on Moffett's (1968) developmental theories of audience distancing and abstraction. In this model, occasions for writing increase in difficulty, moving from concrete to abstract in four domains: (a) mode, (b) genre, (c) cognitive complexity, and (d) distance from audience.

In early stages, students wrote informally, keeping personal journals, primarily for themselves, in order to begin thinking about the issues they choose to research. In the course of developing an idea, they shared their writing with trusted friends, and conducted partner research via a less personal stance. Small collaborative groups drafted reports, and as research partnerships expanded, so did the audience for the work. Ultimately, one of the opportunities offered by the Civic Engagement Project's partnership network is that peer reviews can be conducted across school sites and that Kentuckians across the state serve as a ready audience for final projects.

The role of art and media in critical literacy and civic education is to make public the ideas of young learners, giving voice to their understandings and developing perspectives (Hirzy, 2011; Howlett, 2010). When learner-centered education extends beyond the classroom, it becomes a public endeavor that includes not only how students learn (process) but also what they understand (product).

Media Design and Production

From the public library to the stage of the local theater, students interact with the larger community, develop compelling performances, and communicate their findings via dialogic and aesthetic media. Siblings, elders, neighbors, and local officials serve as an audience for the student work, and as such, are made aware of critical issues, then, in turn, become more motivated to take action. In doing so, they too grow as civic leaders in their own right. Multi-modal literacy and a belief that the arts are fundamental on multiple levels—not the least being a means of human expression and representation—inform the project's performance aspect.

Although Adrian created a painting to represent her new insights on racial segregation in her community, more often students in the Civic Engagement Project choose to render their insights in digital media. To date, students have created websites, Facebook pages, digital videos, and storybooks to express their perspectives and represent the information they found. In so doing, learners have had to think carefully about forms of representation that would express their concerns effectively. Additionally, these students engaged in composing forms of information (text, image, and sound) in space (virtual or real) to educate and motivate members of their communities.

Such complex activities of learning could be daunting if presented in traditional *stand and deliver* ways. In this project, however, the messages learners *made public* were personalized through student choice and real-world application. These eighth-grade students cared deeply about their topics, were proud of what they learned, and became passionate about sharing that new knowledge in an effort to compel others to action.

The civic engagement curriculum invites learners to consider a range of art forms—music and composition, dance and choreography, the visual arts, and audio-visual media. Partnering with local artists, musicians, playwrights, and storytellers, students are exposed to a wide range of options for expression and representation, as well as exemplars that inspire them to think larger.

Project Partners

Public education is a participatory community endeavor. Schools do not exist as stand-alone agencies but rather in community contexts that include numerous constituents. As such, innovations that extend beyond initial efforts more often occur in partnership with a wide range of individuals and groups.

From philosophic, to strategic and naturally occurring school and community partnerships, the Civic Engagement Project invited adolescents to utilize action-research methods to address real-world critical issues in their home/local communities, then work with other partners to turn their research into public performances (see Table 4.2).

From the outset, rapid formation of the interdisciplinary team was crucial. Team membership expanded with full participation of higher education and state department of education partners balanced with participation from artists and other practitioners, especially superintendents, principals, and teachers. In later phases, less common partners signed on, including diverse agencies, organizations, and individuals. From the Richard Dreyfus Foundation, Project Citizen, Kentucky Educational Television, EvaMedia Inc., and the Woodford County Historical Society, to musicians, photographers, printmakers, and students, we welcomed everyone.

A collaborative, creative, and scholarly community focused on civic action, student voice, and artistic representation developed. As we engaged in this unfolding curriculum, with input from all partners, it inspired the development of civic dispositions, skill in persuasive writing, and understanding principles of design and production via various media.

CLOSING THOUGHTS

The kinds of innovation needed for 21st century education involve key ideas. Students, for example, must own their learning. They must be given the opportunity to co-create new systems of learning and peer-support and take on roles in advocacy and communication efforts to build connections to the broader community. Drawing on models of participatory democracy (Freire, 2007), the Civic Engagement Project is situated firmly in a framework of student leadership.

From the outset of the Civic Engagement Project, students led in researching and identifying problems and made consensual decisions about format and audience to whom their work would be communicated. In defining community issues, determining the focus of their service, and directing the project's content, they steered the work. In elegant irony, student leadership was foundational to the project's success and increased leadership was a projected outcome.

Other ideas that seem foundational to the Civic Engagement Project are tied to learning that promotes individual growth towards increasingly complex understandings in a space conducive to inquiry, rather than a traditional schooling model governed by time and scheduled measurement. Such a

Kinds of Partners	Sample Partners	Rationale	Suggestions
Leadership partners	University faculty Artist practitioner State Department of Education	The initial formation of such a project requires a leadership commitment from key constituents.	Welcome diverse perspectives on the leadership team.
School partners	Three geographically distant middle schools	Schools were chosen because principals provided full support.	Co-author memoranda of understanding to establish clear goals, roles, and responsibilities.
Teacher partners	social studies teachers	Teachers volunteered to participate.	Encourage teacher teams at each school site.
Student partners	300 8th graders 60 preservice teachers Graduate students	Students from the P-20 community worked together to create change.	Invite participation rather than require it.
Philosophical partners	Project Citizen	Many civic organizations can serve and inform the project.	Take time to share the work of your project.
Professional development partners	Kentucky Center for the Performing Arts Bluegrass Writing Project EvaMedia Inc.	Teachers need access to resources, conversation about the pedagogy, opportunities to learn new media, and colleagues with whom to collaborate.	Make time for teacher inquiry too.
Research partners	Institutional Review Board Parents	Investigating the impact of the project serves as quality control.	Use the data to secure external funding and extend participation.
Other partners	Educational television Local historical societies and arts councils	Naturally occurring partnerships grow from the nature of the students' inquiry.	Find resources to support the work of the teachers and students.

Table 4.2

Collaborative Partnerships for the Common Good

space facilitates learning that is personal, relevant, and full of intriguing possibilities.

Designing and implementing a learner-centered and inquiry-based curriculum challenges authority in fundamental ways. At times it calls on teachers to relinquish control, moving aside while students follow their own intrigue and discover that which is continually unfolding in their lives.

REFERENCES

Freire, P. (2007). *Pedagogy of the oppressed.* New York, NY: Continuum.

Hirzy, E. (2011). *Engaging adolescents: Building youth participation in the arts.* New York, NY: National Guild for Community Arts Education.

Howlett, C. F. (2010). Writing local history journals can be engaging and educationally worthwhile. In A. Honigsfeld & A. Cohan (Eds.), *Breaking the mold of school instruction and organization: Innovative and successful practices for the twenty-first century* (pp. 161–166). Lanham, MD: Rowman & Littlefield.

McCrary, N. E., & Mazur, J. M. (2010). Conceptualizing a narrative simulation to promote dialogic reflection: Using a multiple outcome design to engage teacher mentors. *Educational Technology Research and Development, 58,* 325–342.

Moffett, J. (1968). *Teaching the universe of discourse.* Boston, MA: Houghton Mifflin.

Parker, W. C. (2006). Public discourses in schools: Purposes, problems, possibilities. *Educational Researcher, 35*(8), 11–18.

II

Engagement with Literacy and Language

"It is within the power of every teacher to inspire and motivate students to find a lifetime of pleasure and information in the reading of good books" (Gambrell, 2004, p. 198). This section of the volume addresses the many challenges related to the reading motivation of students from early childhood to college.

Audrey Figueroa Murphy and Robin E. Finnan-Jones address the needs of English language learners (ELLs) and introduce us to the struggles and successes of two 4th grade ELLs who, although they started out as reluctant readers, were given the appropriate support to develop both literacy skills and self-esteem.

Patricia M. Breslin and Rebecca Ambrose take us into the middle school ELL classroom. They explore how *teacherless* discussion may be used to engage young adolescents in the learning process through meaningful, curriculum-driven, peer-to-peer talk about literature and topics of great importance. Beverly S. Faircloth and Samuel D. Miller offer insight into the transformation of a ninth-grade English department, where the teachers collaborated with a university professor to establish ways the students could become partners in designing their own educational experiences.

Evelyn M. Connolly presents technology tools and strategies that not only advance secondary students' literacy development but agency as well. As a result, they are able to take charge of their own learning in the broadest possible contexts. Most prominently, she discusses a digital storytelling project, during which students readily combine traditional reading with Internet research skills and other current technology-based practices.

Meg Goldner Rabinowitz describes a unique set of learning experiences introduced in the secondary language arts classroom that are personally relevant and evoke students' curiosity. Heather Rogers Haverback's chapter reintroduces 21st century college students to reading for pleasure. In sum, the chapters in this section all conclude that engagement with personally relevant and meaningful literacy materials and tasks is needed for student motivation and college and career readiness.

REFERENCE

Gambrell, L. B. (2004). Literacy motivation: Implications for urban classrooms. In D. Lapp, C. Collins Block, E. J. Cooper, J. Flood, N. Roser, & J. Villamil Tinajero (Eds.), *Teaching all the children: Strategies for developing literacy in an urban setting* (pp. 193–201). New York, NY: The Guilford Press.

Chapter Five

Empowering English Language Learners: Reluctant Readers Learn to Believe in Themselves

Audrey Figueroa Murphy and Robin E. Finnan-Jones

PORTRAIT OF A CHANGING POPULATION

Public School 616 sits proudly on a tree-lined street in a densely populated urban neighborhood inhabited by newly arrived immigrants. The area used to be home to working-class families mainly of Italian and Irish descent. Today, of the 1,300 students housed within the school's pink brick façade, 92 percent come from a home where English is not the first language. For most of these youngsters, the primary language is Spanish.

Over 90 percent of the students are at or near the poverty level. Many of them live in rooms containing multiple families, divided by hanging sheets, and sharing facilities such as bathrooms, kitchens, and even sleeping mattresses. In such a scenario of poverty and abject need, parents and caregivers dream of a better life for their children. And they know that the way to achieve this is through education.

The ages of students at the school range from 5 to 13 years old. Many are a year or more behind others their age in formal schooling. Many have not attended school on a regular basis in their native country, due to living too far away or having a pressing need to contribute to the family's income. Some have not attended school at all. Bernabe is such a child, coming from a rural area of Guatemala, having only attended school periodically. Although he is the requisite age for grade four, Bernabe is not yet reading at the first-grade level.

For the first three months of the school year, Bernabe remained quiet, still in the silent period of English language acquisition. More recently, he began to open up, sharing his beginning knowledge of the alphabet and the sounds of each letter. Bernabe told his teacher that his *abuelita* taught this to him at home. Bernabe has a quick smile and speaks rapidly, often swallowing parts of his words in Spanish. For example, instead of saying *hablado* (spoken), he says *habla-o.*

When others laugh at him, he joins them in the laughter, often making himself the center of the jokes, sometimes ridiculing himself in the process. His teacher believes he covers up his insecurity in the school setting with jokes and smiles, often insincere, but necessary for his emotional survival. It is evident that Bernabe does not believe he is in charge of his learning, nor is he convinced that he can learn.

Reina is another student in the same grade. She is tall and appears much older than her actual age of 10. Reina wore party dresses to school for the first month until she noticed that torn jeans were the requisite attire for emerging teens. Reina tries to be brave, and say what is on her mind. She still stands when called upon in class, although she was the only student following this protocol, learned in her native country, but not customary in the United States.

Reina attended the first two years of school in El Salvador and was reading at a beginning second grade level when placed in her U.S. class. She is shy, reluctant to speak aloud in class, cognizant of her accent, of being new, of being different, and of trying to fit in. Since Reina already knows the reading basics, her teacher thinks she can catch up once she masters the language. Reina prefers to speak and read in Spanish, believing English is too hard to learn, and she will never catch up to her English-speaking peers.

THE CHALLENGE

Students such as Bernabe and Reina used to be few and far between; now they are increasing in number nationwide. Many of these students view the learning process negatively because they never learned the basic concepts taught in earlier grades. Being on the fourth grade level, students in Bernabe's and Reina's classes are devouring books containing intricate literary language and more complex vocabulary without the need for extensive pictorial support.

There is a shift from graphophonic analysis to a greater need for comprehension and meaning analysis. If students such as Bernabe and Reina do not grasp initial reading concepts, the higher order thinking required of upper grade students will be difficult, if not impossible to develop. This may cause them to feel frustrated, unmotivated, and unable to engage with their peers or instructors.

The teachers at this school wanted to help their students but were at a loss as to where to begin to address areas of difficulty. English as a Second Language (ESL) educators especially felt all eyes were upon them to solve this challenge. Listening to the talk in the teachers' lunchroom, one could sense that their self-esteem was plummeting as ESL teachers grappled with diagnosing where the learning was breaking down and how to engage their students in meaningful instruction.

KEEPING STUDENTS ENGAGED AS THEY PROGRESS TO GRADE LEVEL

As Bernabe stumbled over many words in a story from a first-grade reader, he often lost the thread of meaning along the way. When Reina read aloud, it was apparent that she was having difficulty navigating the current text. As these students learned the English language and wrestled with reading concepts, what could be done to not only support them, but to inspire them? How could they be empowered to take ownership of their learning and believe in themselves and their abilities?

The English as a Second Language (ESL) teachers knew it was up to them to take the next step. They decided to form a study group along with the classroom teachers to tackle the problems confronting their students. Issues—such as a lack of a formal education and below-level reading—all pointed to a need to reinforce early reading skills. Realizing that students must be fluent and able to comprehend books, they began digging into the research on reading instruction.

The Report of The National Reading Panel (National Institute of Child Health and Human Development, NICHD, 2000) identified one of the major goals of reading instruction as ensuring that students become fluent readers; consequently, teachers identified repeated reading as a key strategy for improving students' fluency skills. Studies outlined ways to support students as they read with recorded books and suggested implementing *repeated reading* as a tool for practicing reading (Rasinski, 2003).

Among other researchers, Stahl and Kuhn recommended that students be given the opportunity to reread sentences and receive encouragement as they learned to decode and construct meaning from text (as cited in Kuhn, 2004). A plan was beginning to emerge to teach students necessary skills to develop fluency and to give them ownership in their own learning.

THE PLAN

While examining the data, the study group noticed that with the publication of the *Report of the National Reading Panel* (NICHD, 2000) fluency has been brought to the forefront of reading methodology. The report highlighted two instructional approaches to fluency development including practice in repeated oral reading, as well as an increase in the independent reading students do on their own. However, the additional variable for the school was that this student population was one of English language learners (ELLs), making the task more demanding.

The teachers discovered there were several factors contributing to the challenge. Many of the students came to school without any concepts of print. Therefore, gaining basic text navigation skills was one of the necessary foundations for fluency instruction. Additionally, since many ELLs do not share a U.S. cultural background, they found it difficult to derive meaning from distinctly U.S. cultural concepts or expressions.

Simply decoding the language was a formidable task; deriving meaning from figures of speech without the aid of shared cultural background made the task of comprehension even more difficult. The teachers noted that infusing instruction with American nuances or common idiomatic expressions would greatly assist the cultural as well as the language transition.

Furthermore, the group also agreed that ELLs would benefit greatly from explicit instruction in oral language skills to help them match new sounds and words to print, since oral language fluency supports reading fluency (Gorsuch & Taguchi, 2010). ELLs are often accurate decoders, but if the expressions have no meaning for them, mastery of new words becomes essential to developing fluency. Moreover, as Palumbo and Willcutt (2006) pointed out, students need to become aware that many English words have several meanings.

The teacher group met once a week and came up with a plan to use two intervention methods to increase student fluency and ultimately their comprehension: *Books on Tape* and *Repeated Reading*. Smith and Elley's research demonstrated that students who read and listened repeatedly to recorded high interest stories until they could read them successfully on their own, made an average gain of 2.2 years in reading achievement (as cited in Rasinski, 2003). In addition, recorded reading materials can accompany students to their home for further practice.

PUTTING THE PEDAL TO THE METAL

The time to put these ideas into practice was the present. Teachers volunteered to select small groups of no more than six ELLs in their classes to see if these interventions would engage students with the material and produce subsequent growth in reading achievement. Students participated in the mini-lesson conducted by the classroom teacher with the ESL teachers' assistance prior to the repeated reading session.

Materials were selected at students' instructional level. A picture walk would be conducted prior to the first reading of each book. The book would then be read back to the students while they followed along in their own copy of the book, using their fingers to keep their place in the text, thus making the experience tactile as well as visual. For the second reading of the book, the students would read or echo back the sentences read.

During the third reading, the ESL teacher would stay quiet and listen in as the students read the book out loud to themselves. At this point, the children would read the book together in pairs, each taking a turn in reading to their partner. While they were involved in this procedure, the ESL teacher would call them up, one by one to read aloud, assisting them with words, as needed. The students were instructed to take the book home and read it to a family member, so that each child would have multiple exposures to the book (Doyle & Zhang, 2011).

At the next reading session, another book would be introduced using the same procedure. For the independent reading time, the ESL teachers would hold conferences with individual students, during which the children would read the book aloud, while the teacher reviewed the strategies and assessed comprehension. Additionally, the teachers would hold strategy and guided reading groups as needed during the course of the class. Students began to feel ownership as they became familiar with the new vocabulary, and noticed an increase in their ability to decode, pronounce, and understand the new words and accompanying text. Members of the student groups began to look forward to the sessions and felt motivated to read. They told their teachers that they felt proud to bring the books home and read them to their families, many of whom had never learned to read.

Dividing the students into small groupings was a significant factor in the success of this method. ESL teachers, in collaboration with the classroom teachers, were able to monitor the progress of these students closely through conferencing, guided practice, and strategy lessons. Therefore, the success of each of these participants was truly a joint effort.

REACTIONS TO THE INITIATIVE

A variation of Readers Theatre was used with Bernabe, who loved to be the center of attention. In Readers Theatre (Rasinski, 2003), students stand in front of an audience, usually made up of their classmates, and read from scripts they hold in their hands. Without movement, costumes, props or scenery, the performers have only one attribute to make their performance meaningful and satisfying: their voices. "And, in order to use their voices well, performers must practice the text beforehand" (Rasinski, 2003, p. 105).

The book *Henny Penny* (Zimmerman, 1996) was used as repeated reading and then as the script for Bernabe and his group to perform for their classmates. The students practiced reading the part of their character several times, while paying attention to the punctuation and reading with the character's voice. At the end of the unit of study, the students performed for their classmates in celebration. The students clapped and Bernabe beamed.

The students were very motivated during the repeated reading sessions. For example, Reina was given books that were one level above her independent level of reading. When she was able to read these books to other students in the class, she read purposefully and meaningfully, with her eyes shining and her voice clearly articulating each word.

Reina was given the opportunity to take the books home and practice reading them again. When she came back to school after bringing the books home, she was eager and excited to read the books to her teacher, as well as answer comprehension questions and retell the stories. As the unit of study for the class was woven into the lessons, there was continuous reinforcement of the reading and comprehension strategies needed to read the higher level books. As Reina became a more fluent reader, she became highly motivated, and read more and more books.

IMPLICATIONS FOR ENGAGING RELUCTANT OR STRUGGLING ELLS

What did the school community discover as a result of this initiative? Most importantly, extra support for struggling readers did assist the students in progressing to higher levels of reading. The repeated reading method was an excellent support for ELLs and struggling readers. It was easy to implement within the fourth-grade units of study on which the school was focusing. *Readers Theatre,* which is an adapted form of repeated reading, served as a method of improving fluency, and could be useful for older struggling readers as well.

Listening to books on tape, or on CD-Rom, was a form of repeated reading that could be done without the teacher and, therefore, would increase the number of students who could benefit from this method. Since many parents cannot afford the audio equipment to use at home, the school is now considering opening a lending library to offer the audio equipment (CD players, etc.) and the books on tape to their families, thus enabling the students to listen, to see the book, and to read along. Plans were being designed to hold parent workshops at the local library, thus involving parents in literacy activities and community projects. Computer programs (White & Gillard, 2011) which offer the same type of experience for students and could be used to assist struggling readers were also being considered.

Teachers realized that by reading to students they were able to model and share their own enthusiasm for reading. An additional bonus was the strengthening of comprehension through reading sophisticated texts—texts that students cannot handle on their own. Teachers throughout the school began to support the effort by encouraging students to borrow the books after they had been read in the class, to peruse them together with a partner, or to take them home to examine.

CONCLUSION

As the three o'clock hour nears, students spill out of PS 616 from every conceivable doorway. Parents wait anxiously, holding younger siblings by their hands, eating ices sold from the local street vendors. Bernabe comes out the side entrance and finds his *abuelita* in the crowd of parents, students and teachers.

Bernabe shows his grandmother his certificate of reading progress, awarded to him today by both his classroom and ESL teachers. He shows her the books he is taking home and cannot wait to start reading to her. As he opens one of the books and reads the first page, his *abuelita's* face lights up with joy and pride at his accomplishment. Bernabe says nothing; his wide smile says it all. But this time it is sincere.

Reina comes down the main entrance and is greeted by an older brother who asks how school was today. Reina proudly tells him about her reading progress, and shows him the new, sophisticated books she is taking home over the weekend. She promises her brother she will read one to him each night. He looks at her and knows this can be nothing but the truth.

NOTE

All names are pseudonyms.

REFERENCES

Doyle, A., & Zhang, J. (2011). Participation structure impacts on parent engagement in family literacy programs. *Early Childhood Education Journal, 39*, 223–233.

Gorsuch, G., & Taguchi, E. (2010). Developing reading fluency and comprehension using repeated reading: Evidence from longitudinal student reports. *Language Teaching Research, 14*(1), 27–59.

Kuhn, M. (2004). Helping students become accurate, expressive readers: Fluency instruction for small groups. *The Reading Teacher, 58*, 338–344.

National Institute of Child Health and Human Development (NICHD). (2000). *Report of The National Reading Panel.* NIH Publication No. 00-4769. Washington, DC: U.S. Government Printing Office. Retrieved from http://www.nichd.nih.gov/publications/nrp/smallbook.cfm

Palumbo, T., & Willcutt, J. (2006). Perspectives on fluency: English language learners and students with dyslexia. In S. J. Samuels & A. Farstrup (Eds.), *What research has to say about fluency instruction* (pp. 159–178). Newark, DE: International Reading Association.

Rasinski, T. (2003). *The fluent reader: Oral reading strategies for building word recognition, fluency, and comprehension.* New York, NY: Scholastic.

White, E. L., & Gillard, S. (2011). Technology-based literacy instruction for English language learners. *Journal of College Teaching and Learning, 8*(6), 1–5.

Zimmerman, H. (1996). *Henny Penny.* New York, NY: Scholastic.

Chapter Six

Teacherless Discussion: Engaging Middle School Students Through Peer-to-Peer Talk

Patricia M. Breslin and Rebecca Ambrose

A LOOK AT JON

Seventh-grader Jon was a tough child to reach. A bright, energetic, attractive boy, he spent the majority of his time in the classroom finding ways to entertain himself and his peers rather than work. His teacher at the time, Ms. Breslin, was a first-year teacher who found Jon to be one of her most challenging students. She tried detentions as well as phone calls and e-mails to his parents when his behavior was inappropriate. Despite these efforts, he rarely turned in any homework. In addition to his lackadaisical demeanor in the classroom, Jon was also a student who quickly judged others and a few students reported feeling verbally bullied by him.

When Ms. Breslin learned that she would be looping with her students up to eighth grade English, she felt intimidated about starting a whole new curriculum, and even more worried that she was not effectively reaching all her students, especially Jon. Ms. Breslin was also concerned about creating a safe classroom space for her diverse class. A unit on *The Diary of Anne Frank* (Frank, 1995) provided Ms. Breslin an opportunity to research a new approach to instruction and to show Jon and his peers the value of tolerance and acceptance.

Ms. Breslin's K–8 school educates Hispanic, African American, and Russian immigrant children including many students that are the first generation in their family to be born in the United States, as well as many English language learners. As students enter the middle school, they become acutely

49

aware of their ethnicity and begin to develop their racial identities (Tatum, 1997).

In Ms. Breslin's school this was manifested with students mocking one another, especially in regard to their ethnicities. Consequently, Ms. Breslin wanted her students to stop judging their peers for their differences and learn to listen to one another's point of view. She knew that lecturing them was not going to accomplish that.

FOSTERING SUBSTANTIVE ENGAGEMENT IN DISCUSSION

It was at a 2010 Advancement Via Individual Determination conference (AVID, n.d.) during the summer between her first and second year of teaching when Ms. Breslin found a teaching technique that would take advantage of the loquaciousness of her students like Jon, while also addressing students' intolerance for differences.

She was introduced to the Socratic Seminar (Copeland, 2005), an instructional strategy that actively engages students in a learner-centered class discussion of a text. In this approach, students read a text, develop probing questions of interest, and engage in a group discussion, without the input of the teacher. While the format of this teaching tool was being described at the conference, Ms. Breslin kept thinking, "They get to talk *and* learn? How perfect was this?"

Parker (2006) noted that "seminars encourage students to plumb the world deeply" (p. 12), and he emphasized that group discussions enable students to participate in a culture of listening and speaking to see that new ideas can emerge through articulating diverse viewpoints. Ms. Breslin hoped that by engaging her students in the Socratic Seminar, they would begin to value what they could learn from one another and to appreciate diversity as a resource for their community.

According to Nystrand and Gamoran (1991), substantive engagement depends on authentic inquiry in which participants engage in true dialogue with one another. Genuine questions that students ask of each other are the most likely to be taken up by their classmates and to lead to genuine conversation about topics of interest (Nystrand, Wu, Gamoran, Zeisler, & Long, 2003).

In these interactions, students exchange ideas of relevance to them, exploring the meaning they are making of text and the extent to which their interpretations are shared with others. Despite its power, true dialogue is rare in classrooms (Gamoran & Carbanaro, 2002). Ms. Breslin was intrigued to see the extent to which her students would engage in true dialogue.

Development of Costa's Questions

The Socratic Seminar begins with learning how to ask discussion-provoking questions through Costa's Questions (AVID, 2011), a hierarchy similar to Bloom's Taxonomy. To learn about Costa's Questions, Ms. Breslin had students generate questions about unethical studies in psychology that they had researched and presented to the class. She chose to focus on ethics with this group of students because she wanted them to begin thinking about the way they were treating each other.

When considering the three levels of Costa's Questions, the class learned that answers to Level 1 questions can be found in the text, for example, "Where did the psychologists find Baby Albert for their study?" Questions such as "How were the study of Baby Albert and the study of Jeannie, the wild child, similar?" require inferences and are, therefore, Level 2 questions. The class found Level 3 questions, such as "How would you feel if you had the same experience as Baby Albert?" and "How would these experiences affect you as you grow up?" to be the most challenging and interesting because they required that students integrate their prior knowledge with the text.

Discussion Format

After exploring the Costa's Questions framework, the students moved on to learning about the discussion aspect of the Socratic Seminar. To begin the process, Ms. Breslin challenged her students to develop Costa's Questions at different levels for *The Diary of Anne Frank* (Frank, 1995), which would be used in the discussion the next day. For the exchange, Ms. Breslin divided the class into two sections to promote maximum engagement.

When it came time for the seminar, she had the students push their desks to the perimeter of the classroom and arrange their chairs in two concentric circles. One group was designated the discussion group and sat in the inner circle, whereas the other group observed the discussion and took notes while sitting in the outer circle. One student was asked to start the discussion with one of his or her Level 3 questions. Ms. Breslin was accustomed to controlling the flow of classroom interaction; however, the goal of the Socratic Seminar is to give the students power over their thinking, and consequently their learning.

She found that after modeling appropriate behavior—for example, how not to speak over another student, when to ask a question, or how to respond appropriately without an attacking manner—the students readily adapted to their new roles. Although the students were often rambunctious and outspoken in the formal classroom setting, they were more engaged in learning and acted more respectfully toward each other. One plausible explanation for their appropriate behavior was that they were intrigued by the format and did not want to lose the privilege of participating.

OPEN DISAGREEMENT

Upon reflecting on the first day of the Socratic Seminar, Ms. Breslin noted that her students were very eager to try this new method, especially Jon. He knew that he was finally going to be allowed to speak in the classroom without negative consequences. In fact, he seemed disappointed that he was not chosen to start off the discussion.

In this first session, Jon asked six questions, the first of which was: "Do you think Peter and Anne really like each other, or is it just there is no one else?" He also asked, "So how's Anne and her mother's relationship going to turn out?" and "How do you know if you got called up?" Jon's questions demonstrated not only curiosity about character motivation, but also interest in seeking background information about the time period. Students engaging in the discussion were then able to share their perspectives and knowledge with Jon.

The first seminar was so exciting for Jon that he dominated much of the conversation. He responded 38 times to other students' questions in this seminar. Needless to say, the other students were becoming frustrated with Jon's more than frequent participation, so Ms. Breslin invited them to try and negotiate the flow and organization of their own discussion.

During the seminar, the students debated the risk versus the benefit of adding an eighth member to the Annex, Mr. Dussel, a dentist. Most of the students agreed that the Franks and the Van Daans had a moral responsibility to save as many people as possible. Jon conversely felt that it was too dangerous to allow more people into the Annex and risk the lives of the seven Holocaust victims that already lived there. His justifications included: "Would you rather kill 8 people or 7?" and "What if the dentist brings in disease?" and "The dentist is only a dentist and wouldn't be much help." Because Jon's perspective on the matter differed so greatly from the majority of his classmates, this topic became quite intriguing to all of the students.

Most tried to rationalize with Jon, asking him to put himself in Mr. Dussel's shoes to see if that changed his opinion. Jon, however, held on to this initial interpretation. Ms. Breslin was surprised and encouraged that the students were truly listening to one another. Even though Jon's peers tried to change his beliefs on the topic, they never mocked him for his different perspective. They allowed Jon to speak his mind, which made for a much more interesting and engaging conversation that involved higher order thinking for all participants.

The final discussion was Ms. Breslin's favorite of all the seminars because the students moved away from the history of the Holocaust and began to analyze the conditions of the human spirit as a result of the abuse experienced by its victims. The students began to develop a realistic understanding of the severity of this time period.

In this final discussion, Jon asked, "Why didn't they just steal the guns from the guards and take over the camps?" Another student replied, "Because this was real life, not a video game. In a game, you die and come back to life. In the camps, you just died." Another student noted that even if one person gained control of a gun, "there's a difference between a war and a one-man army."

The students discussed the weakened spirit of the victims of the camp, and how the physical and emotional abuse they had endured would affect their will to survive. Jon noted, "I would die trying to save someone…" He felt very strongly about the duty the people in the camp had to try and save their families.

From his comments, it became clear that Jon was trying to imagine how he would react to being in Anne's situation, thus providing evidence that the Socratic Seminar helped him to integrate ideas from the text with his own life. While most of the students agreed with Jon's belief, others reflected on the dire situation the victims of the camps were in, and how their physical and emotional condition would make it extremely difficult to fight. The students seemed to have grasped the desperation of the Holocaust and were able to move past ideal situations of survival and onto the reality these individuals experienced.

In the two years that she had this group of students, Ms. Breslin had never seen her students as involved in an activity as they were with the Socratic Seminar. She saw her students growing as independent learners, taking control of their engagement with a text, and participating in an academic conversation with their peers. When she administered an end-of-year feedback survey, 33 students expressed enthusiasm for the Socratic Seminar and only one preferred a more traditional teaching style to the seminars.

Ms. Breslin was especially happy with Jon's contribution to the discussion, particularly his willingness to take an opposing position to his peers. It demonstrated an *academic capacity* he had not displayed in traditional classroom activities and he practiced listening to and respecting his peers rather than teasing and taunting them.

REFLECTIONS

Many teachers use standard forms of assessment: multiple-choice tests, short written responses, and formal essays. In her first year of teaching, Ms. Breslin struggled with how to assess the students who had something to contribute and who understood the material but did not have the skill or motivation to put their thoughts in writing.

For a student like Jon, the Socratic Seminar provided a format in which he could demonstrate his comprehension and analysis of some fairly complex material, an ability he would not have been able to demonstrate if asked to write an essay. Jon expressed his appreciation by stating, "I like that we get to talk in class. Usually all we get to do is book work and reports and stuff like that, but with this we get to talk with our friends."

After completing the initial seminars, Ms. Breslin has continued to vary her instructional approaches to promote greater engagement and deeper thinking. She has begun to use Costa's Level 2 Questions because they require students to analyze the text and draw on specific examples from it to make inferences.

Ms. Breslin found that *The House on Mango Street* (Cisneros, 1984) proved to be an effective and thought-provoking reading for the Socratic Seminar because some of her students have had experiences similar to those described in the text. Ms. Breslin continues to look for other relevant selections that promote conversation among her students. She also plans to discuss current events using the Socratic Seminar.

CONCLUSION

Ms. Breslin was gratified with Jon's participation in the Socratic Seminar and was convinced that this instructional approach motivated and engaged him more effectively than other group discussion formats. In general, all of her students began to value one another's input as a result of their interactions. As one student noted during a group discussion about the benefits of the Socratic Seminar,

> When you do this, you think about what you read but then someone else will ask a question about something you've never thought about and you think about your answer and you think more about what you read and it becomes easier to understand.

The students became aware that their classmates had insights that they could benefit from and were appreciative of the diversity of opinions in the class. Ms. Breslin concluded that through the Socratic Seminar her students began to respect one another more and made an important step toward acceptance.

REFERENCES

AVID. (2011). *Arthur Costa's levels.* Retrieved from http://www.avidregion4.org/resources/documents/tutorial/ArthurCosta.pdf

AVID. (n.d.). *What is AVID?* Retrieved from http://www.avid.org/abo_whatisavid.html

Cisneros, S. (1984). *The house on Mango Street.* Houston, TX: Arte Publico Press.

Copeland, M. (2005). *Socratic circles: Fostering critical and creative thinking in middle and high school.* Portland, ME: Stenhouse.

Frank, A. (1995). *The diary of a young girl: The definitive edition.* New York, NY: Doubleday.

Gamoran, A., & Carbanaro, W. (2002). High school English: A national portrait. *High School Journal, 86*(2), 1–13.

Nystrand, M., & Gamoran, A. (1991). Instructional discourse, student engagement, and literature achievement. *Research in the Teaching of English, 25,* 261–290.

Nystrand, M., Wu, L., Gamoran, A., Zeisler, S., & Long, D. (2003). Questions in time: Investigating the structure and dynamics of unfolding classroom discourse. *Discourse Processes, 35,* 135–196.

Parker, W. (2006). Public discourses in school: Purposes, problems, possibilities. *Educational Researcher, 35*(8), 11–18.

Tatum, B. (1997). *"Why are all the Black kids sitting together in the cafeteria?" and other conversations about race.* New York, NY: Basic Books.

Chapter Seven

Staying Afloat in Ninth-Grade English: Letting Students Trim the Sails

Beverly S. Faircloth and Samuel D. Miller

NAVIGATING A SEA OF IRRELEVANCE

At first glance, the high school classes showcased in this chapter appear to contain the standard accoutrements of ninth-grade English: literature selections, writing assignments, discussions, and bored, restless adolescents. Situated in the public high school with the highest dropout rate in their county—one that had not achieved adequate yearly progress (AYP) in over a decade—these remedial and repeat courses contained more than their fair share of struggling and reluctant students.

Classes were characterized by chronic truancy, groaning responses to assignments, noncompletion of homework, and agonized claims that class was boring. Slumped over their desks, many students were either sleeping or well on their way. What was not immediately obvious was the unique path these classes would embark on during this particular year of ninth-grade English.

A frustrated band of six teachers—whether because they had nothing to lose ("Nothing else is working.") or out of total exasperation ("Things can't get much worse.")—made the conscious decision to invite their students to engage as partners in designing their own educational experiences. Rather than penalizing students for overt and nearly constant resistance to engagement in learning, the teachers partnered with a local university professor to attempt to understand what the students needed and why *they* were frustrated.

The *tipping point* (Gladwell, 2002) in this story occurred when one teacher surrendered and asked her students what they meant by their constant refrain that class was boring. The typically semi-comatose class quickly transformed into an energized discussion of their frustration. Their deceptively simple definition of boring—that schoolwork had "nothing to do with *me*"—belied the power that one issue chronicled their engagement in education. By way of illustration, Antoine (all names are pseudonyms) picked up the current piece of literature and asked, "Ms. V, aren't *all* of these characters White?"

Even among such diverse classrooms (45 percent African American, 33 percent European American, 15 percent Latino, and 7 percent Other), the discrepancy between students' lives and experiences—and those represented in their schoolwork—had escaped the notice of their teachers and the researcher. Hungry for any solution to what ailed their classrooms, the teachers latched on to this insight. Literature selections were broadened immediately to include characters and settings whose demographics, culture, and context mirrored those of the students.

A powerful first example was *Bronx Masquerade* (Grimes, 2002), the story of a diverse group of high school students living in the Bronx and studying poetry from the Harlem Renaissance. As the characters in the book developed their own voice in poetry, they also learned more about themselves. Students clung to the opportunity to study literature that reflected their own lives and interests like clinging to a life preserver in a sea of high school irrelevance.

Many—whose typical classroom behaviors earlier in the semester included physical manifestations of the boredom they reported—began to demonstrate interested, involved, and enthusiastic participation, including asking questions, completing assignments, and reporting eagerness to continue to learn. Several students began to carry a copy of this new novel in their back pocket, keeping it close by to be read in their spare time; some asked for their own copy of the book to keep. A small number of students from other classes—having heard enthusiastic reports about this book—requested copies as well.

When asked to account for this transformation, Antoine explained that when he read this book, he could see himself in the story, finding it real, which served as a powerful catalyst for his engagement. His classmates agreed: "I felt like I was there," or "I could see the adventures happening."

By being empowered to negotiate this dimension of their participation in English to reflect their own identity, many students were able to move from resistant, bored nonengagement to energized participation. The six teachers showcased below did not just adopt a new piece of literature through this experience; they also learned powerful lessons about their students. Not only did their students have the capacity to engage meaningfully in classroom learning, they had keen insights into what they needed as students.

CONSTRUCTING LIFE PRESERVERS FOR CLASSROOM LIFE

The growing realization from research that the gap between students' lived and school experiences could be bridged by offering students a voice in the texts, topics, and tasks of their school work (Fairbanks & Ariail, 2006), supported the participating teachers' insights regarding their students' engagement.

Brophy (2008) informed the team's understanding of how to scaffold students' appreciation for learning, by highlighting the intersection between students' identities and their learning experiences as a powerful setting for student engagement. Nisan (1992) echoed this thought, reminding educators that the route to making the curriculum desirable or engaging might best be accomplished through acting "in accordance to one's personal identity" (p. 133).

Flum and Kaplan (2006) explained that students who are taught to intentionally examine the relevance and meaning of school content and learning with respect to their sense of who they are or want to become develop an exploratory orientation toward learning that involves actively seeking and processing information. This research-based perspective suggested that learning is best conceived as being more than engagement in particular classroom activities or the accumulation of knowledge and skills.

Learning involved participatory choices, or the negotiation of one's place in a learning community. That is, student engagement in learning consists in part of negotiating membership within the classroom by receiving, resisting, or revising who they were expected to be, to match who they think they are, or want to be, in that particular setting. McCarthy and Moje (2002) suggested that this process is an attempt by students to create identities or stories that allow them to feel like they belong, or fit, in their school setting; they "just want to be part of the [classroom] story" (p. 232).

Contemporary researchers have suggested various paths through which such connections to learning might be supported. Each draws explicitly on the practice of authenticating students' lived experiences and empowering students to demand such authenticity in their schoolwork. In a study of urban Latino high school students, Moje et al. (2004) found that although students had significant funds of knowledge available to them from their lives outside of school (Moll, 1990), such resources were rarely accessed in the school settings.

Moje et al. (2004) argued that by attending to what is relevant and important to the student, a hybrid identity integrating students' lived and school experiences could be created. Such intersections could disrupt the negative patterns of academic motivation generated by the marginalization students often experienced in traditional school settings.

Lee (2007) agreed that it is the role of schools to understand the resources, skills, and perspectives that students bring to the educational setting and to design learning environments in ways that allowed the differences between community-based and school-based norms to be negotiated by students and teachers. Similarly, Fairbanks (2000) attempted to offer students personally significant reasons to engage in schoolwork by inviting them to investigate topics of their own choosing that had a specific connection to their lived experiences (which she referred to as *kids' business*).

Tan and Calabrese Barton (2008) illustrated strategies for connecting student lives with their learning within a diverse group of adolescent science students. They observed students elevating their engagement in learning when they were allowed to draw from the funds of knowledge (Moll, 1990) inherent in their backgrounds to author new modes of engagement.

When students were allowed to connect their musical knowledge, cultural knowledge, or street smarts with course content—for example, writing and teaching a song about material being studied—many students moved from low levels of engagement to active engagement within one school year. The researchers referred to these outside-of-school knowledge sources as *noncommodified*—that is, although they are directly connected to learning from the students' perspectives, they have not traditionally been given value in the classroom.

DEVELOPING NEW STROKES

Following this line of reasoning, the teachers worked together to explore issues of student identity, culture, and authenticity, as well as to involve their students in classroom conversations about how to scaffold their engagement in learning. They searched for opportunities to allow students to shape their own learning in ways that they found meaningful. Moreover, they asked students directly how to support such engagement. Student suggestions centered around the following four issues:

1. Empowering students with more choice;
2. Selecting literature that reflected students' ethnicities, cultures, and lives;
3. Continually relating school work to students' identity, culture, and lives; and
4. Allowing as many avenues for student voice as possible.

Each of these students' ideas echoed what the teachers were learning from research (Brophy, 2008; Fairbanks, 2000; Moje et al., 2004) and became one of the pillars of their new classroom practice.

In order to capture the events in this chapter and accurately reflect students' perspectives, four of the classrooms in this study were observed by the researcher on a weekly basis for the entire semester. At the end of the one-semester course, participants from all of the teachers' classrooms completed a qualitative survey exploring their perspectives regarding the relationship between their classroom learning opportunities and student engagement. They were asked to address items such as:

- *What activities in your English class have allowed you to relate what you are studying to things that matter to you? What did you like and dislike about these assignments?*
- *Describe an English assignment that you would be willing to devote extra time and energy to and explain why.*

Participants also took part in one individual interview with the researcher exploring in more depth the issues addressed in students' written surveys. This allowed the researcher to further understand students' perspectives (e.g., *What makes a classroom activity "fun" or "interesting"?* [a frequent student claim]).

CATCHING A WAVE

Both students and teachers reported increased interaction with regard to engagement in learning. Weekly observations of class sessions revealed many students moving from marginal or nonparticipation toward more genuine engagement. Nearly every student verbalized the value of relating class content and activities to their *sense of self*, and surprise at being allowed to choose activities and issues that mattered to them. Their stories, as well as their actual choice of words tell it best.

Masks

When the ninth-grade students were invited to individually select books for a final literature project, Davy appeared lost. He explained, "Ms. V., you know I don't read!" His teacher realized that she had the answer at her fingertips when she recalled that although Davy struggled to connect with novels, rock music sprinkled most of his conversations, adorned his clothing, and seemed to fill his head as he drummed nonstop on desktops, doodled, and decorated his notebooks.

When his teacher allowed him to use carefully selected music lyrics as his literature choice, classroom observations found Davy buried under, and engrossed in, stacks of lyrics. Not only was Davy able to forge a strong connection between this learning task and the fact that he viewed himself as highly

invested in music, he firmly resisted engagement until he was able to negotiate this link. At that point, his participation in class moved from being a
frustrated, drifting nonparticipant to becoming an engrossed, eager community member.

Many students described how a connection to self undergirded their engagement, explaining: "I had more space to be myself;" or, "It made you
want to find the story that you have to tell for yourself." Several students also
reported learning about themselves in this process, claiming that the new
classroom activities: "made me feel like I know who I really am" or "make
you understand the person you want to be." As though they were seeing their
reflection in a mirror, students were not only able to determine whether they
recognized themselves within their learning experiences; they also grew to
know themselves better through the process.

Although it would be inaccurate to suggest that the strategies employed in
this study provided a panacea for student engagement, even among students
who remained disengaged, identity played a role. For example, one student
claimed, "In order to 'make it' at this school, I would have to dress differently and be someone that I'm not." The engagement in learning that Davy and
many other students were able to craft was powerfully summarized in one
student's explanation that, compared to this experience, in most classrooms
he was, "wearing a mask instead of really feeling connected."

Amps

Luiz typified the unengaged students in his remedial English class. It was
unusual to find him involved in class activities, when he attended class at all.
Daily attempts by his teacher to encourage his involvement were met with
frustrated claims that the class was boring. However, a visit to class two
months into the semester revealed him to be busy working on a research
project on prison life that he claimed he found important and interesting. As
class ended, he actually sought assurance that he would be allowed to continue working on his project the next day.

What had occurred in the interim was that students had been invited to
select research topics about which they were genuinely passionate. Topics
selected, many of which were common currency in the lives of these students, included depression, divorce, drugs, gangs, abuse, and guns —as noted
in class conversations, student artifacts, and reported out-of-school experiences.

Prison life was a particular favorite for many students who regularly
visited incarcerated family members or had been in adolescent boot camp
themselves, as was the case with Luiz. Attending prison boot camp was a
part of his experience that surfaced repeatedly in how he talked about himself
in class.

Luiz's engagement—and that of many of his classmates—was transformed when students were allowed to explore authentic questions they had about topics that resonated with their lives. In a lesson in contemporary adolescent vernacular, these changes were accurately summarized by one student who explained that, amid the relevance and choice offered in this class, learning was "*amped*!"

Buoys

The partnership between the teachers and students provided clear evidence that even typically disaffected, low-performing students in a high-needs school can negotiate meaningful engagement in learning. Moreover, the pathways to such empowerment involved relatively modest, reproducible strategies that fit within the normal requirements of a ninth-grade English class. This highlights the growing realization that the gap between students' lived and school experiences is not completely intractable (Fairbanks & Ariail, 2006) especially if we engage students more actively as partners in the educational enterprise.

One student offered a rich summary of the impact of these experiences, describing them as a "buoy" to his learning experience. Such was the effect of connecting identity with learning, and the impact of the freedom to negotiate learning practices in meaningful ways: a prop, a guide, keeping some afloat, life-saving for others. Whatever the role, the potential of such opportunities to support students' engagement is well worth the investment of additional research and thought.

REFERENCES

Brophy, J. (2008). Scaffolding appreciation for school learning: An update. In M. Maehr, S. Karabenick, & T. Urdan (Eds.), *Advances in motivation and achievement* (Vol. 15, pp. 1–48). New York, NY: Elsevier.

Fairbanks, C. M. (2000). Fostering adolescents' literacy engagements: "Kids' business" and critical inquiry. *Reading Research and Instruction, 40*, 35–50.

Fairbanks, C. M., & Ariail, M. (2006). The role of social and cultural resources in literacy and schooling: Three contrasting cases. *Research in the Teaching of English, 40*, 310–354.

Flum, H., & Kaplan, A. (2006). Exploratory orientation as an educational goal. *Educational Psychologist, 41*, 99–110.

Gladwell, M. (2002). *The tipping point: How little things can make a big* difference. London, UK: Little Brown & Co.

Grimes, N. (2002). *Bronx masquerade*. New York, NY: Dial Books.

Lee, C. (2007). *Culture, literacy, and learning*. New York, NY: Teachers College Press.

McCarthy, S. J., & Moje, E. (2002). Identity matters. *Reading Research Quarterly, 37*, 228–238.

McCarthy, S. J., & Moje, E.B. (2002). Identity Matters. *Reading Research Quarterly, 37*(2), 228-238.

Moje, E. B., Ciechanowski, K. M., Kramer, K., Ellis, L., Carrillo, R., & Collazo, T. (2004). Working toward third space in content area literacy: An examination of everyday funds-of-knowledge and discourse. *Reading Research Quarterly, 9*, 38–70.

Moll, L. C. (1990). Introduction. In L. C. Moll (Ed.), *Vygotsky and education: Instructional implications and applications of sociohistorical psychology* (pp. 1–27). Cambridge, UK: Cambridge University Press.

Nisan, M. (1992). Beyond intrinsic motivation: Cultivating a "sense of the desirable." In F. Oser, A. Dick, & J. Patry (Eds.), *Effective and responsible teaching: The new synthesis* (pp. 126–138). San Francisco, CA: Jossey-Bass.

Tan, E., & Calabrese Barton, A. (2008). Unpacking science for all through the lens of identities-in-practice: The stories of Amelia and Ginny. *Cultural Studies of Science Education, 3*, 43–71.

Chapter Eight

The Power of Technology to Advance Literacy, Learning, and Agency

Evelyn M. Connolly

With a customized alert from his iPhone, "ring..., get up man, ring...," Zach rolls out of bed and hits the weather icon. Dressing quickly, he hits the Enter key to check if there were any important Facebook messages and leaps down the steps in an energetic mood. This all changes as he remembers his exam in English and the essay he needs to write with his self-noted terrible handwriting. "Why can't I bring my Notebook to school to type the essay?" he thinks as he slows down his pace and sinks into a negative *school mood*.

Zach is no special case. Millennial students, also referred to as the *iGeneration* (Rosen, 2011) have grown up surrounded—and shaped to a great extent—by technology. As digital natives, their out-of-school experiences document a wide range of involvement with multiple forms of communication, particularly those involving technology (Prensky, 2012). They include "being online, using computers offline, listening to music, playing video games, talking on the telephone, instant messaging, texting, sending and receiving e-mail, and watching television" (Rosen, 2011, p.12).

If we were to video students today with a multimodal lens, we might see the student assume a technological *identity kit* (Gee, 1996) rather than a traditional backpack. It is conceivable that by 7:30 on a Monday morning, the video would have captured the *screenager* watching the highlights of the weekend sportscasts on a 50-inch flatscreen plasma TV, sending digital photos via their smartphones and posting details of the event to Facebook, downloading music from iTunes, tweeting, and texting a friend for a ride to school (Scherer, 2011).

Before homeroom, the video would capture a visit to the computer lab where the student would be seen plugging in a USB memory stick to display an essay on the screen, then print it, and file it in the identity kit for later access. During class, students would share impromptu stories written as they had listened to a podcast posted on their teacher's blog. At the same time, although cell phones and iPods are usually restricted from use in class, some students would be seen wearing headphones, most likely listening to music; others communicating surreptitiously with friends via text messaging on a smart phone in their pocket!

THE POSSIBILITIES OF MULTIMODAL LEARNING

In an 11th grade English class, Rob—although considered the most improved student by his teachers for the first quarter of his junior year—had failed a high-stakes test at the end of the second quarter. As a result, his participation in class waned; he avoided assignments, and entertained others with grimaces, comments, and improvisations. However, with the introduction of digital storytelling, a process that involves using multimedia technologies, Rob's interest was piqued and led him to a new level of engagement.

For his research project, he produced a digital story on hip-hop culture, in which he put his thoughts together, visually, aurally, and kinesthetically to tell a story that had relevance to him and to his peers. "There are a lot of images out there that show the impact of hip-hop on culture. There is a lot of music and text out there to explain my culture," he wrote in his response journal. Rob's choice of hip-hop was not surprising since his out-of-school literacy practices included graffiti, music downloading, shopping online for caps and shirts, computer generated graphics, and participation in Web 2.0 interchanges (Connolly, 2008).

The digital storytelling project involved Rob and his iGeneration peers (Rosen, 2011) as competent and capable literacy learners. They were empowered to critically interpret and communicate information and to make choices among a range of media techniques. Their digital stories vividly demonstrated how nontraditional multimodal engagements supported, extended, and changed the ways that they (a) constructed and communicated their understandings, (b) became engaged in class activities, and (c) expressed their personal identities.

The increasing dominance of visual images and technology in today's postmodern world can pose challenges to traditional practitioners, but Kress (2003) noted that in order to participate fully in this culture our students must be able to think, create, critique, question, and communicate effectively using the visual and digital forms they encounter daily.

TRANSFORMATION THROUGH THE INCORPORATION OF NONTRADITIONAL MODES

As reported in the case study, *From Page to Screen* (Connolly, 2008), the digital story project situated students as competent, motivated, and autonomous literacy learners. Their experiences demonstrated how traditional research assignments can be embedded in nontraditional multimodal engagements. Students succeeded as digital storytelling opened the door for them to reveal their expertise and express their personal interests. It provided a context in which their out-of-school literacy practices converged with their school experiences to transform the ways in which they constructed meaning, engaged in classroom activities, and expressed their personal identities.

The following discussion points to the ways that digital storytelling (a) thoroughly engaged the students as they drew upon their personal interests and expertise, (b) fostered within the students a positive sense of personal identity and agency (or the expression of a sense of self) as they repositioned themselves as authors of powerful media compositions, and (c) became a vehicle for students to practice both traditional and 21st century literacies.

ENGAGEMENT CREATED THROUGH CHOICE, SOCIAL INTERACTION, AND TECHNOLOGY

Students needed no prodding to engage in the research project. They participated dynamically as they drew upon their interests and expertise drawn from their involvement with multimodal activities in their out-of-school *lifeworlds* (New London Group, 1996).

As students brought their understandings of Internet searches, image manipulation, and music downloading into the context of the classroom, their learning became intentional, focused, and seemingly effortless. So strong was their motivation that overachievers relaxed and actually enjoyed the experience; apathetic students came to life; resistive students found their own path into the project; frustrated students discovered their self-efficacy; and students for whom English was a second language found their voices.

A significant factor that affected student participation was that of choice, most notably related to design and topic selection. Enthusiastic participation resulted when image creation and music (the two most popular out-of-school activities listed by students in a pre-study questionnaire) were experimented with, combined, and redesigned to create their productions. In the area of topic selection, there were two clear patterns that emerged:

- The ability to use technology for research and representation (vital aspects of their everyday lives) supported the students' choice of topics of personal interest.
- Topic choices reflected the issues relevant in their lives such as violence, teen pregnancy, and drug and alcohol abuse, thereby opening up a personal window that revealed interests and understandings beyond their academic lives.

By experiencing choice, the students took on responsibility for their own learning, which resulted in robust participation. Their performances were marked by independent decision-making and self-regulation. Although their timeline was short, students took the time to *play* with transitions, motion effects, and music to achieve the impression they wished to convey. They were not only in control, but were having fun.

As students shared the enjoyment of working in and with technology, they participated as members of an *affinity group* (Gee, 2003). The computer lab was transformed from a classroom to a workplace where students researched independently, created their own timelines, and often took their work home to develop and polish it for presentation. Thus, the process of digital storytelling wove together the students' personal interests and purposes, technological skills, and social interaction. The multimodal symbol systems afforded them the tools to define and represent their learning and their capabilities as well as fully engage not only themselves, but also, their audience.

IDENTITY AND AGENCY

The importance of affinity groups carried over into the area of identity and agency. During the project, students' *institutional identities* (Gee, 2000) were muted as their identity as Millennials came to the fore. As such, they identified with each other through involvement with technology and its uses, which positioned them as empowered learners.

The opportunity to create a digital story tapped into their strengths and their expertise with Internet searches, image manipulation, and music downloading. They used their research to build their emerging ideas and constructs about social and political realities and to explore issues relevant to their daily lives. This search supported the students' sense of self and positioned them as advocates for themselves and their classmates. Thus, agency was expressed through the use of voice and the creation of counternarratives.

Students were drawn in from the margins and confidently shared their ideas. Introspective students, for whom the writing journal had been the sole audience for emerging values and beliefs, lost their anonymity. Their personal voices, combined with sophisticated images and music, were communicated, understood, and appreciated by a broader audience.

Digital stories that reported on topics such as teen pregnancy, abortion, drugs, and alcohol provided students with a platform upon which to practice taking a stand for future adult involvement and decision-making in social or political issues. This is important because the ability to interpret and design multimodal texts will increasingly be required as students communicate, work, and thrive in the digital, global world of the 21st century.

Hull and Katz (2006) wrote that when students use multimedia in supportive settings that encourage participation, they are empowered to act as "agentive and socially responsible selves" (p. 48). Once freed from the constraints of traditional learning engagements, silent, resistive students, who, like Rob, avoided full participation in traditional assignments, used technology to straddle the divide. They felt empowered to make their own decisions, manage their time, hurdle functional difficulties, and ask for help when needed.

Although challenged at times because of network security filters, the students acted independently, responsibly, and with self-confidence in gathering their research and working with the affordances of the digital storytelling project. They redefined and exhibited their capabilities as they acted to engage and express themselves through multimodal symbol systems.

The students also used the project as a vehicle to promote their self-efficacy, which was a way of "constructing, conveying, and maintaining identity, thought, and power" (Moje, 2000, p. 651). The students identified role models and made personal statements about how they were inspired to pursue their dreams. In a world flooded with icons, the students focused not so much upon the fame, but on the elements of mind, character, and abilities of their role models. Thus, Sherman, an honor student, who admired the poetry of Jim Morrison, spoke to his art rather than to his lifestyle. Additionally, students who were not members of the dominant school culture identified with how their ethnic musical role models achieved success and respect, which may be values of a broader youth culture.

Lastly, the English learners in the class experienced autonomy and agency during the digital storytelling project, which created a space for participation, collaboration, and publication unlike more traditional teaching strategies. These students, often characterized by silence in traditional classroom activities, aligned themselves with their fellow Millennials. Their competence with technology allowed them to demonstrate that they were not empty vessels waiting to be filled with knowledge. Rather, they exhibited knowledge and expertise of subjects of vital interest to them (Moll, Amanti, Neff, & Gonzalez, 1992).

Thus, English learners, whose self-images had been negatively impacted by a first year's experience in an American high school, were empowered to challenge the *American Dream*. As they used media tools to probe American culture, they gained the attention and respect of peers in what became a supportive community (Jenkins, 2004).

Follow-up discussions drew them into conversations in which their oral language was demonstrated to be more than adequate to communicate with peers. Thus, digital storytelling, can be seen as a "hybrid activity that bridged the official and unofficial spaces of both home and school... and invoked novel forms of participation" (Gutierrez, Baquedano-Lopez, & Tejeda, 1999, p. 292). As such, it serves as a model of the kinds of literacy engagements that will actively involve learners in the future.

LITERACY LEARNING

During the digital storytelling project, students readily combined their traditional reading with their competent Internet research skills. As a result, their subject knowledge, sense of story, and vocabulary expanded. Additionally, in composing their written voice-overs, students applied what they knew about good writing—creating strong leads, using details, and adding personal commentary to gain and maintain audience interest.

Students also learned that the format of a traditional research report could be altered as they recontextualized their traditional writing with images, animations, print, and sound. In this way, students abandoned some of the traditional conventions of the research report, primarily, in-text citations.

Rather than being embedded in the text of their spoken voice-overs, sources were listed on a separate *Works Cited* page, and quoted material was highlighted on students' note cards. Thus, students learned the conventions of traditional research reporting but represented them in a manner more appropriate for their multimodal compositions (Jewitt, 2006; Kress & van Leeuwen, 2001; Marzano & Heflebower, 2012).

MULTIMODAL REPRESENTATION

Learning about content was not limited to individual researchers/presenters. Rather, presentations afforded the students the opportunity to use their *audience* skills to learn about and challenge the information presented by their peers. As viewers, they were positioned as *readers* of multimodal texts. They read moving images and listened to voice-over narrations containing information upon which the *producers* wanted them to focus.

Thus, the students drew upon multiple literacies as they navigated different semiotic spheres. For most students, traditional literacy skills and research methods were enhanced during the digital storytelling project. These common core aligned skills included reading for information, taking notes, writing in different genres for a specific audience, and attending to all aspects of the composing process, with particular emphasis on revision. Multimodal representation involved students in utilizing the grammar of visual design (Kress & van Leeuwen, 2001). As they constructed their multimodal texts, they worked within the contexts of materiality, framing, design, and production. As a result, the students became attentive to the following:

- the function of images, music, and transitions;
- the importance of selection and placement of images;
- intentionality in assuring that the interplay of the various semiotic modes produced the intended message; and
- elements of prosody.

Thus, revision was transformed from making changes in a written voice-over text to recursive manipulation of voice, image, sound and action.

CONCLUSION

As the world becomes increasingly global, visual, and technological, it is crucial that the pedagogy in schools acknowledges students, especially adolescents, as experienced meaning-makers in modalities other than traditional reading and writing. As teachers, we are responsible for helping students to be successful both in and outside of school, and for preparing these future citizens to communicate effectively across geographical, linguistic, and sociocultural barriers.

The goal for all teachers should be to help students "to choose the most apt representation for their thoughts and ideas" (Vygotsky, 1978, p. 28), and further develop and enhance their students' potential as makers of meaning, so that they might be fully engaged in their learning and experience empowerment as learners and individuals.

REFERENCES

Connolly, E. (2008). *From page to screen: Multimodal learning in a high school English class.* Hempstead, NY: Hofstra University.

Connolly, E. (2009, July). *Digital storytelling in high school English class.* Paper presented at the Literacies for All Summer Institute. Columbia, SC.

Gee, J. (1996). *Social linguistics and literacies: Ideology in discourses.* New York, NY: Routledge.

Gee, J. (2000). New people in new worlds: Networks the new capitalism and schools. In B. Cope & M. Kalantzis (Eds.), *Multiliteracies: Literacy learning and the design of social future* (pp. 43–68). London, UK: Routledge.

Gee, J. P. (2003). *What video games have to teach us about learning and literacy.* New York, NY: Macmillan.

Gutierrez, K., Baquedano-Lopez, P., & Tejeda, C. (1999). Rethinking diversity: Hybridity and hybrid language practices in the third space. *Mind, Culture, and Activity, 6,* 286–303.

Hull, G., & Katz, M. (2006). Crafting an agentive self: Case studies in digital storytelling. *Research in the Teaching of English, 41*(1), 43–81.

Jenkins, K. (2004). *Social identity.* New York, NY: Routledge.

Jewitt, C. (2006). *Technology, literacy and learning: A multimodal approach.* London, UK: Routledge.

Kress, G. (2003). *Literacy in the new media age.* New York, NY: Routledge.

Kress, G., & van Leeuwen, T. (2001). *Multimodal discourse: The modes and media of contemporary communication.* London, UK: Routledge.

Marzano, R. J., & Heflebower, T. (2012). *Teaching and assessing 21st century skills.* Bloomington, IN: Solution Tree Press.

Moje, E. (2000). To be part of the story: The literacy practices of gangsta adolescents. *Teachers College Record, 102,* 651–690.

Moll, L. C., Amanti, C., Neff, D., & Gonzalez, N. (1992). Funds of knowledge for teaching: Using a qualitative approach to connect homes and classrooms. *Theory Into Practice, 31*(2), 132–141.

New London Group. (1996). A pedagogy of multiliteracies: Designing social futures. *Harvard Educational Review, 66*(1), 60–92.

Prensky, M. (2012). *From digital natives to digital wisdom: Hopeful essays for 21st century learning.* Thousand Oaks, CA: Corwin Press.

Rosen, L. D. (2011). Teaching the iGeneration. *Educational Leadership, 68*(5), 10–15.

Scherer, M. (2011). Screenagers: Making the connections. *Educational Leadership, 68*(5), 7.

Vygotsky, L. (1978). *Mind in society: The development of higher psychological processes.* Cambridge, MA: Harvard University Press.

Chapter Nine

It's All About Me; I Mean You; I Mean Me: Strategies for Engaging Students in the Language Arts Classroom

Meg Goldner Rabinowitz

A pristine aluminum pyramid with a distinctive white strip like a banner. (Zach)

It reeks of preservatives and artificial flavors; the pure, serene, sensual essence of cocoa is nearly unidentifiable. (Liz)

It looks like some sort of Christmas decoration. If I celebrated Christmas, I'd hang them from the tree somehow. And we'd all know Christmas was over when the tree lay bare, stripped of its sweet candy, perhaps trampled on in some depraved soul's feverish attempt to find the last remnants. (Jesse)

Hershey's kisses are shaped as tear drops. Does this signify something? (Julie)

I'M IN 11TH GRADE... IS IT RELEVANT TO ME???

When faced with the question of how learning can be made relevant to students, teachers can engage students by establishing frameworks that invite students' fundamental level of curiosity. Using curiosity as a student motivator can be traced back to the early writing of Dewey (1938), in which he stated,

> If an experience arouses curiosity, strengthens initiative, and sets up desires and purposes that are sufficiently intense to carry a person over dead places in the future, continuity works in a very different way. Every experience is a moving force. (p. 38)

For instance, the simple strategy of slowing down the process of observing allows students to interpret the world in ways they may have never done before. In the activity quoted above, the students examined a simple pair of Hershey's kisses and were provided with categories for writing down their observations. This was an invitation for the students into the process of inquiry.

As teachers, we often ask ourselves, how do students construct meaning? We question students as to what patterns can be detected in their descriptions. Which sense was the most vividly described? How does the process of carefully and critically examining the Hershey's kiss inform the students' experience of eating the kiss?

In this successful and interactive example, the teacher brainstormed with the students about each of the senses and generated a clear listing and understanding of sight, smell, sound, touch, and taste, so that the students could begin the work of enhancing their observations. For several students, the kiss was a wonderful springboard which led to an elaborate sensory memory or imagined scene. Julie continued,

> Hershey's kisses are shaped as tear drops. Does this signify something? Love is pain, kisses are tears. In the television advertisement for Hershey's kisses, the voiceover asks two posed kisses, "What happens when you kiss a kiss?" One wrapped kiss grabs another, pulls it close, and embraces it while the voice on the television announces, "It blushes." And the kiss that was kissed turns progressively from its natural silver color into a red tinfoil.

In an effort to further extend the learning experience, students were offered opportunities to free write and create news stories, poems in any form, or prose descriptions based on the material they have compiled in their observations (and the shared observations of their classmates). How wonderful would it be to introduce students in a 10th grade English classroom to Heisenberg's (1949) *Uncertainty Principle* about objects being observed changing because they are being observed? How does the act of thinking about eating chocolate and carefully delineating the process of eating chocolate *change* the way one eats chocolate?

BROADENING OUR SCOPE

In what is an enormously helpful theoretical framework for engaging student learners across disciplines, Lytle and Botel (1990) suggested that there are four lenses for examining language, literacy, and learning in students. Rather than seeing the study of literature as singularly text-based, teachers can situate their approaches to encompass a wider range of meaningful academic and intellectual endeavors, all under the larger heading of *Language Arts*. In

Table 9.1, each of the four lenses Lytle and Botel identified—Lenses of Focus—is described, explored, and then elaborated upon based on teaching experiences that may emerge as a natural outgrowth of each approach (Application).

LANGUAGE EXPLORATION IN THE BROADEST POSSIBLE SENSE

The study of language arts does not manifest itself in only one of these lenses or contexts, and there are both fundamental differences and unifying experi-

Lytle and Botel's Lenses of Focus	Specific Quotes from Lytle and Botel to Support or Explain Each Lens	Application of Lytle and Botel's Lenses to Successful Teaching Strategies
Lens One: Language is a Way of Making Meaning	"Effective readers, writers and speakers use language actively and constructively to gain new ideas and insights. Language can be a powerful tool for relating the new to the known, for making the concepts of a subject one's own, and for becoming aware of what one does and does not understand – the latter a metacognitive process that is viewed as essential to becoming an effective and independent learner." (p. 5)	The literature and language arts classroom is an ideal context for students to practice making meaning of the world through the texts they encounter. The introduction of themes, characters, and plots from a range of authors and traditions enables students to become readers of the world and its patterns.
Lens Two: Language is Inherently Social	The second leThe second lens asserts that language is "inherently social, that language use occurs in a situation, and that learning takes place in the context of a community of learners. We make meaning in collaboration with others." (p. 5)	There is potent inquiry about self, family, school, neighborhood, and broader global contexts – the second lens invites students to consider the role of language in each of his or her spheres of influence.
Lens Three: Language Processes (Reading, Writing, Listening, and Speaking) are Inter-related	The third lens suggests the "interrelationships of language processes – of reading, writing, listening, and speaking – each of which is enhanced by use of the others. To learn to read, one needs to write in a variety of genres and for many different purposes. To write, one needs experiences with reading, thereby gaining knowledge of the world and knowledge of the possibilities inherent in written language." (p. 6)	By considering the intersection of where the language students read can shape the language students use to talk or to write encourages a useful hyper-consciousness that is the potency of this lens. Students can re-write their school's published policy for what is acceptable spoken language in their own words.
Lens Four: Language is Inherently Human	"Readers and writers bring their own prior knowledge and belief systems which they orchestrate in ways unique to themselves. Through active use of language in the learning process, students' own voices and styles can be expressed and encouraged, while at the same time explorations of similarities and differences contribute to understanding the perspective of others." (p. 6)	This lens serves as the foundational idea that language classrooms are the perfect setting for examining social justice issues, identity issues, and issues around power. In this lens, students are valued as being readers of the world, of its codes, its contexts, and its messages both subtle and overt. It is this lens too that suggests that a successful experience in learning language arts can empower students to be lifelong and productive readers of the world.

Table 9.1 *Lenses for Teaching Language Arts*

ences that make language in each of these contexts rich and worthy of exploration.

Consider the following literacy experiences:

- reading an example of a sonnet from each of the past four centuries;
- writing a villanelle to understand structure or meter;
- hearing a spoken word poem to understand tone; or
- reciting a memorized Greek choral ode of poetry to understand how the Greek chorus communicated central plot points to the audience.

All would fit under the category of studying poetry—but which one is the fundamental language arts experience? The lenses encourage us to consider all of the approaches.

What Lytle and Botel (1990) inspire the classroom teacher to do is to consider each approach, each plan, each text, in light of the ways in which it invites and allows for language exploration in the broadest possible sense. A vocabulary lesson can become an exercise in meaning-making (Lens One); if students gather, research, and share their definitions, then the exercise also becomes about sharing the range of definitions available (for example, in Lens Two: Language is inherently social).

In response to Lytle and Botel's (1990) first lens where learning is about meaning-making, there are several approaches to presenting material that engage students and invite them to use language to describe their experiences. In a palpable experiment, as described above, the teacher placed two Hershey's kisses on each student's desk. For this exercise, the more the English classroom can be made to feel like a chemistry laboratory, the better. The goal of the exercise is to invite students to make formal observations about the Hershey's kiss—concentrating on and describing each of their sensory responses to the object.

If one combines the framework of Lytle and Botel with Bloom's taxonomy (1956), one finds a rich set of theoretical parameters for constructing a language arts classroom. If one wants to test the inter-connectedness of modalities of communicating (Lens Three), one can ask students to rewrite one of Toni Morrison's sentences as a tweet (140 characters), as a text message, or as a posting on a blog. Students may be intrigued to consider what is lost and what is gained in this exercise, being mindful that an author like Ernest Hemingway convincingly told a short story in six words, "For sale: baby shoes. Never worn."

In the fourth lens, language is inherently human; students are invited to consider that the study of narrative, the study of literature in any of its forms, is a way of becoming familiar with lives outside of their own, lives that share human commonalities at the same time that they reveal astounding differences. C. S. Lewis is attributed the saying: "We read to discover that we are not alone." It is through the fourth lens that students can cultivate empathy, compassion, and a sense of being connected to the broader world outside of the boundaries of their classrooms.

The basic pedagogical assumption is that students learn best when teachers can effectively and productively engage them in rich, multilayered discussions about what they are learning. To expand to another meta-cognitive level, students can also become conversant in how they are learning and where they are learning and begin to make connections in patterns and strands between what they are learning.

CREATING A CLASSROOM OF INCLUSION FOR ENGAGEMENT

Early on in the formation of a productive class, it is useful to establish community norms and to build trust among students and with the teacher. One way of cultivating this trust is to consider overtly the idea of identity with students and to contemplate the ways in which some facets of our identity empower us with agency and some components of our identity make us susceptible to being targeted. Beginning with a table created from student data, the *identity framework* is a highly adaptable graphic organizer that encourages each student to consider his or her own identity from multiple perspectives. Students can begin to see themselves in a variety of contexts and begin to question if each is a facet that is rewarded or invisible, celebrated or marginalized, at different times.

Identity Framework

Once students complete the identity framework chart, they are each given a jigsaw puzzle piece. Each student decorates his or her jigsaw puzzle piece with the five to seven most important components of his or her identity. These can be shared with classmates and posted in the classroom. To build on this exercise, there is a myriad of ways to connect students to each other and to their own experiences. The literature classroom is a rich environment that continually offers opportunities for students to consider complex issues of character development in fiction while building on the language and exploration of identity that begins with the students' own experiences.

In engaging students, we as teachers must meet them where they are, in the heart of their own very personal, very real, very vivid, and very subjective experience of and in the world. For example, in teaching texts where the idea of bullying looms large—such as Philip Roth's (1959) compelling short story, "The Conversion of the Jews" or ancient Greek playwright Sophocles' (2012) great social justice play *Antigone* or even controversial works such as William Shakespeare's (1992) *The Merchant of Venice*—students bring a wealth of their own experiences in encountering bullying to the reading of the text. It is through these classical works of literature that teachers are able to further engage and guide students so that the reading experience becomes meaningful.

Classroom teachers can engage their students in sharing the students' stories of bullying through three fruitful lenses—as victims, as perpetrators, or as bystanders—with thanks to Ozick's (1992) excellent piece about bystandership, the prologue to a collection of sketches titled *Rescuers: Portraits of Moral Courage in the Holocaust*. Though Ozick suggested a fourth category, heroes, those who actively disrupt the forceful cycle of the perpetrator, students can more readily identify in one of the first three categories listed.

When given a square white piece of paper, students can anonymously describe a personal memory with bullying, from any of the three perspectives described. In two hundred words, students can recount examples that range from mildly annoying to harrowing and damaging. No student has ever put his or her pencil down and said, "I have no experience with what you are describing."

Once students have completed the writing, the squares can be posted in an array of a Bully Board quilt. The teacher can then distribute Post-it notes to each student and ask them to respond to three to five different responses, given the amount of class time available. This version of a gallery walk with feedback can be quite powerful and frames the experiences of bullying in a personal, relevant, and community context.

In this exercise, as in any, the best work that the teacher can do is to establish a trusting classroom environment, empower students to give voice to their experiences, invite them to use language to articulate their connection to someone else's experiences, and bring vital and valuable voices from a wide literary canon to shed light on the broader human experiences, the ones that exist far beyond the walls of any one classroom community.

MEANING MAKING AS THE END GOAL

In any of the approaches suggested in this chapter, the guiding principle remains the same: How can teachers engage students in rich discussions and activities that begin with a compelling invitation to consider larger questions on an individually relevant level? So it is not "all about me" or "all about you" but all about both intrinsically.

Before a student can reasonably be asked to consider the literary features, styles, and strategies that any given author employs, each student must feel that the author is accessible, relevant, and contextualized in such a way that brings that author's perspective to life and into focus for the student. This is possible to achieve in a myriad of ways. The classroom can be a rich crucible for exploration, experimentation, critical thinking, and analysis, once a teacher has created a classroom environment:

- where students are learning to make meaning from literature;
- where students are interacting with each other and deriving meaning from that experience;
- where students see that forms and approaches to language—in its many increasing manifestations—are linked to each other and to meaning making; and
- where students are presented with a range of human experiences as reflected in the literature.

Students are inherently teachable, coachable, and able to be engaged. From the moment school begins to the end of the day, the role of the teacher is to invite each student into the classroom and create a safe environment for experimentation, creative leaps, curiosity, inquiry, and reflection to take place (Marzano, Pickering, & Heflebower, 2010). Nurturing each of these vital tasks in learning requires trust, organization, and creativity from the teacher.

The pursuit of knowledge as an end goal is vastly different than the fostering of intellectual imagination that begins with one's own experiences of the world and applies them to the broader contexts one encounters in any rich curriculum, across disciplines. The idea that a student can set his or her personal interests aside and embark on an authentic educational experience vastly underserves the student. Scientists can explain how cognition works and we know that enlightened self-interest, a powerful tool that can be harnessed in adults, is also a driving force in adolescent development. Why not begin there?

REFERENCES

Bloom, B. S. (1956). *Taxonomy of educational objectives: The classification of educational* goals. Chicago, IL: Susan Fauer Company.

Dewey, J. (1938). *Experience and education.* New York, NY: Macmillan.

Heisenberg, W. (1949). *The physical principles of the quantum theory.* Mineola, NY: Dover.

Lytle, S., & Botel, M. (1990*). The Pennsylvania Framework for Reading, Writing, and Talking Across the Curriculum (PCRPII).* Harrisburg, PA: Pennsylvania Department of Education.

Marzano, R. J., Pickering, D. J., & Heflebower, T. (2010). *The highly engaged classroom.* Bloomington, IN: Solution Tree Press.

Ozick, C. (1992). Prologue. In G. Block & M. Drucker, (Eds.), *Rescuers: Portraits of moral courage in the Holocaust.* (pp. xi-xvi). New York, NY: TV Books.

Roth, P. (1959). *Goodbye Columbus.* New York, NY: Vintage International.

Shakespeare, W. (1992). *The merchant of Venice.* New York, NY: Washington Square Press.

Sophocles. (2012). *Antigone* . Hollywood, FL: Simon & Brown.

Chapter Ten

Everything Old Is New Again: 21st Century College Students as Engaged Readers

Heather Rogers Haverback

WALKING THROUGH A CAMPUS

While walking through a 21st century university library, one may be surprised to see the number of books being read in contrast to the number of laptops, smart phones, and tablets being used for research. While a few students may have their nose in a book, the vast majority is fervently texting, e-mailing, or Facebooking with their friends; the click of a keyboard is more prevalent than the turning of a page.

Today's college libraries are not necessarily the home of the book anymore, with fewer and fewer funds being allocated for buying new books. For example, an alumni newsletter from a large flagship school recently boasted that 80 percent of their financial resources were allocated for e-resources. Thus, much library funding is supporting technology, including e-resources and "the social."

This trend is coinciding with another emerging and concerning trend; adolescents and young adults are losing the drive to read books for pleasure. Recently, Mokhtari, Reichard, and Gardner (2009) found that 85 percent of undergraduate college students reported they prefer spending time on the Internet more than they enjoy reading for pleasure, reading for courses, or watching television.

Together, these trends may leave one to wonder whether or not this absence of reading books is a negative trend. An argument could be made that reading an actual book for pleasure is antiquated, and should be left for past generations, much like listening to an eight-track tape. However, one could argue that the activity of reading literature is worthwhile for a number of reasons, especially with today's e-reader devices which enable reading for pleasure with great accessibility.

First of all, while reading is important for individuals of all ages to learn and comprehend new information, reading literature as opposed to text messages is crucial to developing and maintaining one's ability to comprehend complex written information. Second, reading is central to those who will become teachers, as it is enjoyable not only to perform but also to teach, and when brought back to university students, it may become not only a hobby for them but a passion that they can bring with them to the classroom.

IS READING FOR PLEASURE REALLY IMPORTANT?

There is an emphasis on children's reading ability, as it has been noted that reading is vital to one's development and aspects of one's life (Holden, 2004). While this focus is found in the schools, it is also noticeable in many other aspects of our culture. When one turns on the television, many of today's children's programs focus on reading, letter knowledge, and sounds. Likewise, toys and video games are marketed as tools that can help a child learn to read.

While the focus of beginning reading seems pervasive throughout society, it is all but extinct from the adolescent and young adult realms, which is worrisome for a number of reasons. First of all, there has been an improvement in reading scores for younger students; however, these scores decline steadily throughout middle and high school. Further, high school and college students are not reading for pleasure, which coincides with poor reading comprehension and economic consequences (National Endowment for the Arts, 2007). Therefore, one may wonder what an engaged reader looks like and what the benefits of reading for pleasure truly are.

Engaged readers are people who read consistently and with enthusiasm for numerous reasons (Guthrie & Anderson, 1999). However, only a small number of college students would fall into the engaged reader category. This lack of engaged reading is based on the fact that college students are not reading literature, poetry, or fiction as much as they were in years prior (Applegate & Applegate, 2004; National Endowment for the Arts, 2004).

Recent findings from the United States Department of Labor (2011) revealed that full-time college students spent 3.6 hours a day on leisure and sports activities, which did not include reading. While college students have been found to focus their reading tasks on coursework, reading for leisure is not as common (Burgess & Jones, 2010). Perhaps college students would argue that reading for pleasure is not crucial in today's multimedia culture; however, it has been found that reading comprehension scores for high school seniors are also on the decline and United States students ranked only 15 out of 31 industrialized nations on reading scores (NEA, 2004).

A dearth of reading is only further compounded when we consider the fact that tomorrow's youngsters who will be learning to read will be taught by today's nonreaders. How can a six-year-old learn to love reading when the person teaching them to read cannot demonstrate their love for it? This is comparable to being taught statistics by someone who does not enjoy or study statistics themselves. In essence, learning from one who does not enjoy or practice a domain can lead to students lacking the same gumption for the domain. Research shows that student motivation to read is cultivated by teachers who also like to read (Gambrell, 1996).

In contrast, by learning to read with a teacher who loves reading, the students would be more likely to love reading themselves. While elementary schools have reading teachers and literacy experts, those educators may understand reading but not necessarily enjoy or find time to read for pleasure, or model reading for enjoyment. Moreover, research has found that the pre-service teachers' literacy scores correlate with their reading habits and thoughts about reading (Benevides & Peterson, 2010).

Furthermore, such reading teachers may not exist in high schools where content area or other collaborative teachers may be expected to assist struggling readers. This could also perpetuate the current cycle we are describing wherein we have a lack of students who read for pleasure. In turn, these students may become the same preservice teachers who will enter the classroom without a love of reading. As we know, this lack of interest in reading has also been found in in-service teachers (Nathanson, Pruslow, & Levitt, 2008); these same students may become in-service teachers who do not read.

So, what is happening to these nonreading students? In a word, they can be described as alliterate, which refers to a capable reader who decides not to read (Scott, 1996). While troubling, this lack of reading is not surprising. Today's college students are living in the social media of texting, Twitter, and Facebook. Likewise, high-stakes testing, the focus on teacher accountability, and meeting the needs of individual students make teaching more multidimensional than ever before.

The decline in reading for pleasure may leave teachers and teacher educators asking themselves what they could do to organize a classroom that promotes motivation and engagement in college students to read for pleasure. With the knowledge that reading motivation can be enhanced in children through *challenge, choice*, and *collaboration* (Gambrell & Morrow, 1996), these three principles can be used as a guide in creating motivated older readers. This chapter will describe how a professor organized time in a course to allow for college students to become *reengaged* in reading for pleasure.

SETTING THE STAGE FOR READING

During the first class meeting each semester, Dr. Craig, a reading education professor, would ask the students about books they had recently read. Since the course was based on reading, and the students were preservice teachers who were going to soon be teaching children to read, he assumed they would read themselves. However, time and time again, blank stares would fill the room. Perhaps one student would offer up having read *The Hunger Games* (Collins, 2008) that summer. But besides that, crickets could be heard outside of the classroom.

After a few semesters of this trend, Dr. Craig went a step further and asked the students why they were not reading. The overwhelming response was, not surprisingly, time. These students did not feel that they had enough time to read for pleasure. While the course was filled to capacity with state required objectives, it was clear that time needed to be carved out for these students to read for pleasure in order to reengage them.

THE COURSE AND THE READERS

To start, the course under discussion was a reading course for preservice teachers. The syllabus focused on young children's language development, as well as the relationship between language and reading acquisition. In this course, students learned models of reading acquisition and the major components of reading including reading motivation and attributes of a skilled reader.

The students who typically enrolled in this course were at the end of their sophomore or beginning of their junior year. All of the students were poised to be early childhood or elementary education teachers within the next two years. In other words, they would soon teach and motivate preschool, elementary, and middle school students to read.

THE CREATION OF A READING LIBRARY

A few months before the new semester started, Dr. Craig asked a number of friends, colleagues, and family for any used books they were discarding or willing to donate. The books were organized by genre and a small library was created in his office. The students were made aware that this library existed for their use, and they knew that there was an open-door policy for them to come up to the office and borrow a book anytime before or after class.

Books were also brought down to class and selected passages were occasionally shared with the students. While integrating these book excerpts into the class, an interest in the book was generated among the students. This was successful many times, as students would ask to borrow or "look at" the chosen literature.

Creating Reading Time

Despite the academic freedom in a university classroom, Dr. Craig felt he must set aside time to allow for reading literature to take place. The inspiration to organize a group of preservice teachers who read was twofold, and while this plan may seem rudimentary it was surprisingly new to the 21st century students. First, students were given *read for pleasure time* (RFPT) in class. Second, book clubs were implemented. By creating reading time using these approaches, Dr. Craig was also able to use the motivational factors set forth by Gambrell and Morrow (1996).

First, the students were given a *challenge* and asked to read books they had not yet read. Second, the students were allotted a *choice* in what they read. Finally, the students *collaborated* with their peers in reading and discussing the books. It was exciting for Dr. Craig to break the mold and compel these 21st century students to put down their keyboards and reengage in reading. A description of the students and organizational plans are offered in the following sections.

Reading for Pleasure Time (RFPT)

The first task at hand was to remind the students that they could enjoy reading. The idea behind RFPT is that if students are reengaged in reading, they may be more likely to make additional time in their busy days for it. As Dr. Craig is an engaged reader himself, he was more than happy to discuss the books he loved, hated, and wanted to read but had not yet.

During RFPT, the students brought a book to class to read for pleasure for 30 minutes a week out of the 150 minutes of class time. Students had complete autonomy over the books they chose; however, books assigned for another course were not allowed. If a student did not have a book, he or she was invited to come to the reading library to borrow a book. Oftentimes, students would borrow a book and like it so much that they continued to read it.

While part of this plan was a labor of love, it was also an opportunity to be a reading model. Therefore, during the reading time, everyone in the room was quiet and reading together. In an effort to be a good reading model to the students, Dr. Craig brought his own book and read as well. A natural love of reading was demonstrated by Dr. Craig in hopes that the students would be willing to emulate the modeling in the classrooms they will lead in a year or two.

Book Clubs

During another semester, Dr. Craig started book clubs. His desire to introduce the college students to book clubs stemmed from his personal experience with similar literary discussions. Over the years, he had witnessed himself and other individuals become members of various book clubs within which they stayed devoted and engaged. Some of the positive attributes of belonging to a group of dedicated readers is that one is introduced to and responsible for reading a book one may not have chosen otherwise. Likewise, individuals have the opportunity to discuss and build upon their understanding of the readings by discussing the book with their peers. This sharing of ideas is only further promoted by the fact that the group is of one's choosing, so individuals should feel safety in expressing their thoughts and ideas.

The book clubs began by engaging the entire class in discussing different genres of literature. After the discussion, Dr. Craig gave students the opportunity to choose a book club by genre based on individual interest. Each club included five students. Based on the genre, the club members collectively chose a book from which to read. In this case, the reading of the books took place on the students' own time; however, they were responsible for adhering to the timeline chosen by the club. Class time was used to discuss aspects of their books.

Oftentimes, Dr. Craig would pose a guiding question, much like those at the end of novels, which directed the discussion in terms of character development, connections to life, thoughts on the setting, and other literary devices. At the end of the course, participants of the book clubs discussed their thoughts on the reading material.

READING REFLECTIONS

During the RFPT and book club experiences, the students wrote reflections and discussed their ideas with their groups or others in class. The first theme Dr. Craig found throughout these reflections was that most of the students enjoyed the process and stated they felt motivated to reengage in reading. One student stated the following: "I enjoyed the book so much that I read the whole book in a week." In fact, approximately 75 percent who participated in reading book clubs stated that they "forgot how much they missed reading." Another student mentioned how she had forgotten about her favorite author and now she was going to catch up on his books.

A second theme that was consistent in the students' responses was that while reading their books, they found more time to read. One student stated that, "I was able to take my book with me to the doctor's office." Perhaps by picking up a book or e-reader the student realized that the time she usually spends texting or talking on the phone could also be spent performing another pleasurable activity, reading. In fact, many new technologies have been created that will assist in motivating students to read literature for pleasure. By talking about and modeling the use of the Nook, i-Pad, or Kindle in class, 21st century students may feel current.

A third theme that was consistent in the reflections was that the students considered using literature circles in their future classrooms when they become teachers. While time is spent on RFPT in schools today, book clubs are not as common for college-aged individuals. A number of others also stated that reading for pleasure better prepared them to teach reading, and perhaps a piece of that teaching will be incorporating book clubs or literature circles into their own classrooms.

Now they can speak to their future students through the eyes of an engaged reader, not just a teacher. In line with past research that found that dialogic approaches are important in the classroom for a number of reasons including socializing individuals into different ways of thinking (Reznitskaya et al., 2009), students really enjoyed discussing their books and thinking with others.

For many of the students, this was the first time they had engaged in talking about a book. Collaboration helped them reengage with reading, as many reported that they were considering starting a book club with their friends during time usually reserved for web surfing or texting.

CONCLUSION

One student said it best when she stated, "All it takes is the motivation to read one book to get me addicted to reading again." Dr. Craig believed that allowing students time to read literature in their media-savvy lives could really spark an interest in reading again. The students were able to rekindle their interest in reading for pleasure because of this innovative experience integrated into a teacher preparation course. In other words, by offering *challenge, choice,* and *collaboration* along with the time to read (Gambrell & Morrow, 1996), what these students lost in the middle and high school years was reinvigorated in the college years by reengaging in reading for enjoyment.

REFERENCES

Applegate, A. J., & Applegate, M. D. (2004). The Peter effect: Reading habits and attitudes of preservice teachers. *The Reading Teacher, 57,* 554–563.

Benevides, T., & Peterson, S. S. (2010). Literacy attitudes, habits and achievements of future teachers. *Journal of Education for Teaching, 36,* 291–302.

Burgess, S. R., & Jones, K. K. (2010). Reading and media habits of college students varying by sex and remedial status. *College Student Journal, 44,* 492–508.

Collins, S. (2008). *The hunger games.* New York, NY: Scholastic.

Gambrell, L. B. (1996). Creating classroom cultures that foster reading motivation. *The Reading Teacher, 50,* 14–25.

Gambrell, L. B., & Morrow, L. M. (1996). Creating motivating contexts for literacy learning. In L. Baker, P. Afflerbach, & D. Reinking (Eds.), *Developing engaged readers in school and home communities* (pp. 115–136). Mahwah, NJ: Lawrence Erlbaum.

Guthrie, J. T., & Anderson, E. (1999). Engagement in reading: Processes of motivated, strategic, knowledgeable, social readers. In J. T. Guthrie & D. E. Alvermann (Eds.), *Engaged reading: Processes, practices, and policy implications* (pp. 17–45). New York, NY: Teachers College Press.

Holden, J. (2004). *Creative reading.* London, UK: Demos.

Mokhtari, K., Reichard, C. A., & Gardner, A. (2009). The impact of internet and television use on the reading habits and practices of college students. *Journal of Adolescent and Adult Literacy, 52,* 609–619.

Nathanson, S., Pruslow, J., & Levitt, R. (2008). The reading habits and literacy attitudes of inservice and prospective teachers: Results of a questionnaire survey. *Journal of Teacher Education, 59,* 313–321.

National Endowment for the Arts. (2004). *Reading at risk: A survey of literary reading in America.* Retrieved from http://www.nea.gov/pub/ReadingAtRisk.pdf

National Endowment for the Arts. (2007). *To read or not to read: A question of national consequence.* Retrieved from http://www.nea.gov/research/toread.pdf

Reznitskaya, A., Kuo, L., Clark, A., Miller, B., Jadallah, M., Anderson, R. C., et al. (2009). Collaborative reasoning: A dialogic approach to group discussions. *Cambridge Journal of Education, 39*(1), 29–48.

Scott, J. E. (1996). Self-efficacy: A key to literacy learning. *Reading Horizons, 36,* 195–213.

U. S. Department of Labor. (2011). *American time use survey.* Retrieved from: http://www.bls.gov/tus/charts/chart6.pdf

III

Music, Movement, Arts, Drama, and Other Creative Engagements

In a recent publication, Caldwell and Vaughan (2012) noted what many others—including us as editors and numerous contributing authors of this volume—have also observed, namely, how more and more students are becoming disengaged from schools. A plausible explanation they offered was that "school systems are trapped in a traditional model of schooling that is ill-suited to the needs of the twenty-first century and to the ways young people learn in a globalized, high tech knowledge world" (p. 2). This troubling trend is further exacerbated by the pressures of "the unrelenting focus on literacy and numeracy and preoccupation with national tests" (p. 135).

In response to the hyperassessment movement that has begun in the 21st century propelled by NCLB (2002), many educators and parents recognize that their youngsters do not succeed, do not show adequate growth, or do not complete graduation requirements. What has also been found is that (a) establishing an environment that fosters student creativity to flourish, (b) nurturing students' self-expression, and (c) inviting students' authentic voice in the classroom may all lead to heightened levels of student engagement. Chapters in this section offer varied successful documentary accounts of how this can be accomplished in diverse school settings.

Mara Sapon-Shevin's chapter presents several examples of successful interactive teaching strategies that increase student engagement. Eve Bernstein, Anne Gibbone, and Ulana Lysniak describe the use of *Active Gaming* in a middle school physical education class. Vinesh Chandra, Annette Woods, and Amanda Levido introduce an after-school robotics program in

Australia with the purpose of enhancing students' information literacy skills, which in turn, may affect traditional literacy skills.

Joanne Kilgour Dowdy and Mary T. Toepfer illustrate how imaginative dramatic play allows students to be fully engaged in the learning process by stepping into pictures and music scores. Finally, Rut Martínez-Borda, Pilar Lacasa, María Ruth García-Pernía, and Sara Cortés-Gómez describe both the process and the outcomes of turning a music classroom into a rock stage by using both virtual and real instruments. While each of the chapters showcase a different form of art, music, or creative activity, they all successfully demonstrate the positive influence of student-centered, arts-based educational opportunities.

REFERENCE

Caldwell, B., & Vaughan, T. (2012). *Transforming education through the arts.* New York, NY: Routledge.

Chapter Eleven

Increasing Student Engagement Through the Implementation of Interactive Teaching Strategies

Mara Sapon-Shevin

It has been well documented that most learners are more successful when their teachers engage them in active and interactive teaching strategies rather than relying on "chalk and talk" and traditional ways of "delivering" content (Gardner, 1999; Meyer & Jones, 1993; Sapon-Shevin, 2010; Udvari-Solner & Kluth, 2008). The ways in which many teachers were taught, however, and learned to teach themselves lead them to revert to lecture and more teacher-centered strategies as their primary forms of instruction. This is particularly problematic for:

1. Students for whom the language of instruction is not their first or most comfortable language;
2. Students who are or *feel* marginalized for any of their identities (ethnicity, religion, race, class, sexual orientation, etc.), and are less likely to participate in more formal instructional settings;
3. Students who have a history of school failure or struggle which makes them reluctant to raise their hands, ask questions, or participate actively; and
4. Students whose learning styles are not compatible with an emphasis on listening, taking notes, and then repeating information presented in a lecture.

Although this would appear to be primarily a pedagogical issue, it is also a matter of *social justice* and responsiveness to diversity.

When a professor says, "Diversity issues never come up in my class," and even claims that "The Asian students in my class rarely talk—but that's not my fault—I call on anyone who raises his hand," he fails to address students' histories and experiences which might lead them to *not* raise their hands. His assessment of the participation discrepancy as outside his purview also eliminates the possibility of drawing back the camera lens and asking, "Are there ways in which I am currently organizing my teaching that decrease or limit student participation and/or promote the perpetuation of current patterns of discrimination and marginalization?" "How could I change that?"

It has been documented that teaching that is more active and interactive allows all students to accomplish the following:

1. Participate in the learning process, rather than limiting involvement to a small number of students who are willing, eager, or comfortable volunteering.
2. See one another as sources of information and support. It promotes a cooperative atmosphere in which students enact the reality that "together we are smarter" and eliminates competition which can be a major deterrent to full participation.
3. Share their current knowledge so that instruction can be authentically based on what students already know and understand and which can therefore be adjusted quickly and responsively to correspond with students' current understanding of a topic. As such, it is a form of constructivism, in which students are active participants in their own learning and meaning-making.
4. To view themselves and one another differently, able to recognize and appreciate different contributions and realize that there are many ways to be "smart." Thus it can reduce stigma and challenge stereotypes that students (and the teacher) have about who is intelligent and whose knowledge matters.

This chapter shares four active/interactive teaching strategies that have successfully been used across grade levels, instructional settings, and content foci. All of the strategies have the following in common: (a) a focus on ascertaining and surfacing student knowledge; (b) a commitment to promoting positive student-to-student interaction and providing the opportunity for peer support and teaching; (c) the need for relatively little preparation time for implementation; (d) the explicit valuing of student diversity and knowledge, and the reduction of the role of the teacher as "all-knowing" and the only source of teaching and support in the classroom.

HOW TO BEGIN

It is difficult to ask students to engage in learning activities in which they are visible (and vulnerable) if they do not feel that they are valued and appreciated members of the classroom community. Before any *formal* instruction is organized, the teacher must work to establish ground rules for classroom interaction and a mutually supportive learning environment.

Here are three strategies I have used at all levels in order to have students experience voice equity (we hear from everyone), equal visibility and inclusion (we don't leave anyone out), and the development of student-to-student connection.

News and Goods

Start the class by having students say something that is "new" or "good" in their life that they are willing to share. All other students are expected to listen respectfully and without comment. When this activity is first introduced, students may begin by sharing more trivial news, "I saw a good movie on TV last night," "I had a great dinner last night."

As community is built and students trust one another more, they may share more meaningful parts of their life: "I reconciled with an old friend;" "My partner and I just learned that we're going to be able to adopt a baby." News and Goods should never be structured competitively (no prize for the best), and comparative statements ("Well compared to what Mike just said, this is no big deal!") should be gently discouraged.

When a student is having a particularly bad day (or week) and says, "Nothing good has happened," or "I have nothing positive to say," classmates can be encouraged to respond with sympathy and support. It is very important that students *always* have the option to pass and that this is emphasized consistently.

Two Truths and a Lie

Have every individual write down and then share three statements about themselves—two of which are true and one of which is a lie. One at a time, students share their three statements and the rest of the class is asked to guess which statements are true and which one isn't. For example, I might say, "I'm a vegetarian, and I love to cook," "I can ride a unicycle," and "I learned to read Spanish before I could read English." After everyone who wants to has made a guess: "I don't think you could ride a unicycle," or "Your background isn't Spanish, so why would you have learned to read it before English," or "I'm pretty sure you are a vegetarian," I am asked to share the truth (about which I will keep you guessing!).

The critical component of this activity is that it allows people to reveal things about themselves that they are willing to share, but they are not forced to reveal any particular item in any particular area. A student who is shy and not yet comfortable with the group may stick to more superficial facts (and lies) about himself. At a later point in community development, a student might risk sharing more personal information.

Because students themselves get to choose what they share, they are unlikely to be embarrassed or put on the spot. The activity also pushes participants to go beyond stereotypes and assumptions: The student who doesn't *look* like he studies karate may, in fact, be very skilled; the student who others see as shy or quiet may be the one who performs country and western music with her family on weekends.

Stand Up, Sit Down

The teacher calls out a category and asks all the students who belong to that category to stand up (if the class includes students with mobility difficulties, students might raise their hands instead or hold up a yes or no card). Then she calls the next category, and students in that category stand up, and students who are standing from the last category sit down if they no longer are members of the new category. It is possible to engage students in this activity at many different levels. A first-grade teacher began with simple categories: Stand up if you have an older brother; like ice cream; like cats.

For older students, the categories may be more revealing, and as trust grows in the classroom, students can be asked to call out the categories themselves; this can serve as a way of their finding out who in the class feels the same way about something, has had a similar experience, or has something in common with them. Possible categories might include the following: Stand up if you like hip-hop music; are caring for an older relative; if you are nervous about taking this class. This activity can allow students to feel less isolated and to find areas of commonality and connection. Again, it is important to stress that students can choose to pass.

ORGANIZING INSTRUCTION TO PROMOTE INTERACTION

When students feel that they are in a safe environment—they know they will not be teased or made fun of, and they feel close connections to their classmates—it will be easier to implement teaching and learning strategies that are more active and interactive. Here are four I have used extensively with all age groups and across the world, including South Africa, Spain, Chile, Finland, and Australia.

(1) Think-Pair-Share

The Strategy

This strategy is designed to have students think individually, then share with a partner, and then with the whole group.

1. Begin by placing students with partners. You can use a variety of methods to match the students—matching stickers; playing cards (two Jacks who find one another, etc.); little slips of paper with numbers (two people have the same number).
2. Ask students to think about a question and write down their responses.
3. Have students share their responses with their partners.
4. Call the group back together and ask for a report-out from the partners. This can be done either by asking each person to say what they wrote or by asking each person to report what their partner said. They can also report any questions of issues that came up as they were comparing their answers.
5. Record student answers on the board or on chart paper and discuss the results with the class.
6. If appropriate, discuss how the class can find the answers to any questions that came up when they were comparing their responses.

The Possibilities

This strategy can be used to have students discuss almost anything. Any content that can be described, listed, organized, ordered, or sorted can be the focus of the individual and then partner work.

1. Science: Have students make a list of appliances that use electricity; ways to save water in the community; building materials; astronomical facts; geographical formations; alternative energy sources; nocturnal animals.
2. Social Studies: Have students make a list of famous women; countries in Africa; alternatives to war; events associated with World War II.
3. Language Arts: Have students write down synonyms; their favorite character in a particular book; words that can be used to describe a meal; contractions; their favorite part of a story.
4. Social Skills: Have students write down ways to stop an argument; compliments you could give your friends; things you are good at; things you need help with; a time someone encouraged you.

An Example

While attending a conference on Inclusive Education in Santander, Spain, the organizers noticed that very few of the attendees were asking questions or interacting with the materials being shared. In order to change this pattern and encourage more interaction, they asked each speaker to pause periodically in his or her presentation and ask the participants to discuss a particular question with someone sitting next to them. After they had spoken to one other person, they were far more willing to ask their questions more publicly.

(2) Pass the Brainstorm

The Strategy

This strategy is an excellent way for the teacher to find out what students already know about a topic so that they can continue with appropriate activities and further instruction.

1. Have each student take out a piece of paper.
2. Ask a question of the group and have each person, individually, record his or her response on their sheet.
3. After about one minute, have each person pass his or her paper to the person to their left (or establish a pattern that will result in the papers circulating smoothly).
4. The person who receives the paper looks at what is written on it and adds his or her additional information to the sheet.
5. If the person wrote down an answer on the original sheet and that answer *isn't* on the new sheet they receive, they may add it.
6. Repeat steps 3 and 4 about four or five times.
7. After a sufficient number of "passes," regroup as a class and have each person share what is on the paper in front of him or her.
8. If a student has something on his paper that he didn't write, he may still share it.
9. Students who have knowledge that others don't can be encouraged to share that *they* made that contribution and what it means or how they know it.
10. The teacher can make a list/lists on the board of what the students say.
11. After the knowledge of the group has surfaced, the teacher can assign additional research topics, ask students to write about what they've learned or in some other way have students engage with the material that surfaced.

The Possibilities

Students can be asked to write about any topic: all the words you can think of that start with a "J"; things in the classroom that are rectangular; people, events, terms and places associated with the Civil War; ways to decrease violence in society; famous scientists and their discoveries; Asian writers, and so on.

An Example

When introducing the topic of the Civil Rights Movement, I asked students to write down people, places, terms and events associated with that movement. Because the ages/experiences/backgrounds of the students varied widely, the information gathered was diverse. After the lists had been generated, we made four columns on the board and wrote down the responses. It was interesting to see that while almost everyone had written down "Dr. Martin Luther King, Jr." very few students had written "Malcolm X." This occasioned a conversation about why we learn or don't learn what we do, and who or what controls the curriculum.

The activity also provided the opportunity for extensive peer teaching. If one student has written something others don't know, then that student has the opportunity to share her experiences and knowledge. The activity provides a way for the teacher to find out what students already know and to move on from there, and it can also allow mistakes to be exposed and addressed. For example, when one student wrote down "Harriet Tubman," we were able to discuss the fact that Harriet Tubman had lived about 100 years earlier, but that she was definitely *related* to issues of civil rights.

Students with limited knowledge are still able to participate fully, even if they write the same thing on every paper. At the end, they are sitting with a "full" paper in front of them and can contribute those ideas even if they did not write them down originally.

(3) Response Cards

The Strategy

This strategy allows every participant to make a response and for the teacher to quickly assess student knowledge, understanding, and opinion. It is both an assessment strategy and a teaching strategy.

1. Give each person 3-9 cards, each of which has a different "answer" on it.
2. Ask questions that can be answered with one or more of the cards.
3. Have each person hold up the card with their "answer."

4. Ask one or more of the card holders to explain their choice.
5. If there are discrepancies, explore those with the group.
6. If desired, have each pair of participants share a set of cards and make a selection cooperatively.
7. It is also possible to allow participants to generate a question for the rest of the group to answer.

The Possibilities

For any content area in which things can be sorted into different groups or categories, make a card with each category on it. For example, in studying astronomy, students could have cards that said: "moon," "sun," and "planet" and possible questions might be: What do we typically see during the day? Which of these has phases? A lunar eclipse involves which of your cards?

A lesson on nutrition could involve giving each person cards with the following written on them: protein, carbohydrates, sugar, and fat. Questions might include: Tofu would be an example of a food rich in what? Which of these should you eat in limited quantities? Olive oil is a what?

Questions can be designed that have specific "right" answers or they can involve opinions. For example, after reading *Charlotte's Web* (White, 1969), students might each have cards that said: Charlotte, Wilbur, Fern, and Templeton, and the teacher might ask, "Which character do you most identify with?" or "Who do you think was the most resilient character?"

With very young children, the response cards might simply be a smiley face and a sad face, with questions such as "When someone tells you that they really like the picture you made, how do you feel?" or "How do you feel when someone tells you that you're not their friend anymore?"

An Example

In a workshop on disability humor, studying the ways in which jokes and cartoons could be either oppressive or liberatory, each participant was given three response cards: "Funny," "Not Funny" and "Not Sure." My co-presenter, Robin Smith, and I showed them cartoons and asked them to give their response. It was possible to very quickly to see the range and distribution of responses because the cards were color-coded. If there was agreement (i.e., everyone thought a joke or cartoon was funny), we asked several people to explain why they thought that. If there was disagreement, people who had different opinions each explained their thinking, and the ensuing conversation was always illuminating.

(4) Numbered Heads Together

The Strategy

This strategy promotes conversation among participants and ensures individual accountability, because each member of the group must be able to answer the question.

1. Put participants in groups of 3–6.
2. Have each student in the group choose a number (in a group of four, there will be a 1, a 2, a 3, and a 4.)
3. Ask a question of the groups.
4. Have the groups discuss the answer and come to a shared answer that they are ALL comfortable with and can each explain.
5. Roll a die or make slips of paper with each number on it and draw one.
6. If you draw or roll a "2" (for example), ask the number 2 person in each group to stand and then give you the group's answer.
7. Ask another question, allow time for discussion and then roll the die and choose another number to respond.

The Possibilities

This strategy is highly adaptable. Participants can be asked very easy or very complex questions. First graders might be asked to come up with a list of five fruits and vegetables. Sixth graders might be asked to write a story problem involving multiplication and be required to come up with an answer. High school students might be asked to name four places in the world where there was a war going on.

It is important to stress that the student whose number is called is the one who must answer. Group members have not done their job until/unless every member of the group is comfortable giving and explaining the group's answer. This requires peer teaching and support so that every member understands and can report the group's response.

An Example

I gave a workshop in South Africa for a group of teachers who each had 100 students in their elementary class. I had to model strategies that they could use in their large classes. I placed them in groups of six and asked them questions such as "What is the northernmost country in Africa?" and "What languages are spoken in South Africa?"

CONCLUSION

These strategies for building community and teaching interactively will not magically transform a classroom nor lead immediately to more engagement, but they will help students to be involved, interacting with others, and integrating their own knowledge with what is being presented. Equally important, interactive teaching strategies can help students to see one another as smart, capable, and able to contribute, all of which are critical requirements for building a democratic, involved citizenry in which people work well with and support one another.

REFERENCES

Gardner, H. (1999). *Intelligence reframed: Multiple intelligences for the 21st century.* New York, NY: Basic Books.

Meyer, C., & Jones, T. B. (1993). *Promoting active learning: Strategies for the college classroom.* San Francisco, CA: Jossey-Bass.

Sapon-Shevin, M. (2010). *Because we can change the world: A practical guide to building cooperative, inclusive classroom communities.* Thousand Oaks, CA: Corwin Press.

Udvari-Solner, A., & Kluth, P. (2008). *Joyful learning: Active and collaborative learning in inclusive classrooms.* Thousand Oaks, CA: Corwin Press.

White, E. B. (1969). *Charlotte's web.* New York, NY: Dell.

Chapter Twelve

Competition and Considerations: The Use of Active Gaming in Physical Education Class

Eve Bernstein, Anne Gibbone, and Ulana Lysniak

At Sea Shore Middle School (a pseudonym), picture a gymnasium with individual stations and display screens scattered throughout. The lights are low. There is the sound of muffled music and students' laughter, as excited voices fill the gym. Students, wearing their physical education attire, excluding sneakers, are jumping, dancing and moving with excitement, laughing, and interacting with peers at the various stations that are set up with television screens.

Why does this gymnasium look so different from a regular physical education lesson? It does because students are participating in an active dance gaming lesson. Active gaming (AG) can be defined as using technology to engage in forms of movement or exercise. The students are animated as they leave the gymnasium. They are excitedly talking about the fun they just had during the lesson and what they would like to experience in their next AG lesson for this unit.

Using AG is new to physical education programs; Sea Shore Middle School has recently introduced it into its curriculum. For instance, during one AG unit, dancing is used to enhance the physical activity level and socialization. As each class enters the gym, students pick up their fitness report card and proceed to the center circle near the main projector screen for instruction. The physical educator reviews the concepts and strategies for the session, and then students go to their stations and begin the planned activity. Teachers structure practice, so that every student has a chance to improve.

The primary participants, the students linked to the equipment at individual stations, can follow the display on their screens, trying to mimic the moves; for each correct move they receive a point. The secondary participants practice by shadowing their movements behind them, so they can demonstrate proficiency in the moves before becoming the primary participant. The secondary participants are able to work on the entire dance.

Students at each station regulate the order of play by taking turns. Primary participants have the ability to select an individual performance level using the video controller. Students also have the choice to join a group dancing station in the center of the gym to practice. Once the active dance session is complete for the primary participants, they quickly record information on how they did during the session, their scores, or fitness information.

Students then switch roles with the secondary participants, who can record their personal information. After the physical activity has ended, the class rejoins the center circle for a debriefing and a cool down. Each student places the fitness information for that class in their folder as they leave the gym.

Sea Shore Middle School physical educators suggest that the daily focus can change during the AG unit and does not have to have a focus on fitness. An alternative to a fitness focus might involve competition where the unit is structured by the physical education teachers and a competitive game is played. AG that is played competitively is spread throughout the large gymnasium, or is organized within a small space and played in single or multiple player modes.

During the AG unit at Sea Shore Middle School, students compete against a computer-generated opponent or against classmates, while attaining instant feedback. By broadcasting the game on the main projection screen, larger class sizes are easily accommodated. This feature eliminates direct individual feedback, yet projector screens allow practice for more students. When the large projector is used, students at Sea Shore Middle School also have the option to challenge their teachers to games if they choose. Students at smaller stations can challenge other students and record their winnings during this competitive play. The students with the highest total points earn a place on the *Wall of Champions* with their photo proudly displayed.

Whether the focus is competitive or noncompetitive, the teachers at Sea Shore Middle School use AG as a motivational and supplemental teaching tool. Many students are familiar with AG; thus, teachers realize that it can be used to inspire their students in the gymnasium (Gibbone, in press). This is apparent as students talk about the moves that they have learned even after the class has ended. The students discuss what moves they like and the moves they will use again. AG *can* encourage students to try new activities that they have never played before. Students can share their interests in exploring activities outside of the gymnasium, as they practice AG with friends or at home, outside of the school context.

ACTIVE GAMING AS AN OPTION

AG is used at Sea Shore Middle School to teach fitness development and personal fitness planning. The latest trends for children include active video gaming activity at home and/or school to decrease the amount of sedentary time in daily living. When AG is used for fitness at Sea Shore Middle School, students learn the functions of the technology equipment and the relationships that can be made to health-related fitness content and motor skill acquisition. Many of the fitness-focused active games provide users with on-screen information based on their performance, such as calorie expenditure, duration of play, or intensity level, that are recorded in students' personal fitness logs.

This information is discussed, so students learn about health-related fitness and apply it to daily life activities. Mainly, students are engaged in light-to-moderate intensity of exercise during the AG session. Students choose their level of play and intensity. During higher intensity sessions, students can achieve cardiac benefits, depending on the type of game and the vigor expended by the individual.

There are other examples of how schools like Sea Shore Middle School are using AG. For example, video cycling is implemented in the fitness/weight room as a station activity during physical education class time. In addition, AG is the main focus of social- and exercise-related activities in school fitness clubs. Students in the fitness clubs can sign up for a before- or after-school time period to participate (Saslow, 2009).

APPLYING ACTIVE GAMING IN THE GYMNASIUM

Active Gaming can enhance appropriate practice and physical effort when thoughtfully planned and organized. The physical education teachers help students increase control and competence. For example, they may ask the students to pair up with someone who is playing at the same skill level to encourage an exciting competition.

Students overwhelmingly enjoy playing when scores are close between competitors, and when they compete against a classmate with the same skill level. When participating in AG, students select the skill level of play within each specific game. The physical education teachers agree that students choose the levels that match their current abilities, and they make the level more difficult when they feel ready.

Control can be manipulated by the students in AG by pausing and repeating activities when needed. Additionally, they are given an option to go from situations of more control to less control, by first starting out with the projection screen as practice, and then moving on to individual playing stations.

The appeal of AG is that both teachers and students can receive information on the intensity or skill level being worked on by looking at the screen.

COMPETENCE, CONTROL, AND COMPETITION

Active Gaming is programmed to enhance the teaching of competitive sports depending on the design and intention of the game (Lieberman & Donner, 2008). Within many games, there are options for practice sessions or alternative activities that focus on improving accuracy, application of strategies, single versus multiple players, and more. The objectives of the game, and the amount of physical exertion, are tailored to the students' skill levels, goals, and the competitive activity itself (Ryan & Deci, 2000). This amount of control might not be an option in competitive situations that occur during a traditional class activity.

With AG, students increase personal control to provide an appropriate transition into more advanced competitive situations. Competitiveness is regulated by the player, in recognition that low skill students are not able to execute skills if the level of difficulty increases too quickly (Portman, 1995). For example, if students want to take on a greater challenge with increased odds for failure, they choose a level beyond their perceived abilities. Conversely, students choose a level that they are confident in to increase self-esteem. By having a level that challenges their abilities within a competitive situation, the students may accomplish greater proficiency.

Gaming structures are set to promote competition, or remove competition, based on the format selected. Newer games that are being introduced to students at Sea Shore Middle School allow for small or large group participation without the need for each student to have a remote control device for the game, which gives students more freedom to move. However, the students then participate without knowing their performance score or the scores of others. If remotes are provided and available, students can keep track of their scoring, which is intrinsically motivating for some students.

AG eases participation in a sport where anxiety and fear of body-to-body contact or injury may occur. When the element of physical contact is removed, it may be extremely gratifying for students with concerns during traditional sport play. Having the lights lowered makes practice less embarrassing for the students since mistakes are less noticeable to others.

Competitive AG is different from the usual competition in other class activities, because it is "only a game" rather than high stakes competitive play. It is possible that when student perceptions of external pressures are alleviated—such as physical contact, fear of injury, peer pressure, or the embarrassment of looking awkward—widespread student enjoyment can be attained.

Students with low skills have an opportunity to learn rules and strategy in AG, influencing self-efficacy and the potential for continued participation, if interest and understanding of the competitive activity is developed. Students may be more inclined to experiment with new and different sports that they were first exposed to in AG. For example, following the dance AG unit, Sea Shore Middle School students inquired about adding other social dancing to their program. As students are exposed to and become more comfortable with different skills, they may be inspired to seek actual play in addition to gaming in the virtual atmosphere.

ACTIVE GAMING: A NEW AND PROMISING FRONTIER

Sea Shore Middle School is one successful example of how teachers and schools are using technology to enhance instruction. Today, students take part in a myriad of sport and competitive activities during physical education classes. When they participate in these competitive activities in physical education classes, some students have more advanced skills and some do not. Students' success, or failure, in physical activities can be quite public and embarrassing for low-skilled students (Carlson, 1995; Portman, 1995).

If students have both competence and control over a task, the motivation for continuing in that task could be increased (Roberts, 2001; Ryan & Deci, 2000). It is, therefore, important that the competitive activities offered are structured to increase competence and student motivation (Bernstein, Phillips, & Silverman, 2011).

Teachers have the opportunity to incorporate effective strategies that may increase student interest and success (Lysniak, 2010). This is crucial, as physical education classes may be some students' only sources for being physically active or learning about certain physical activities. Teachers at Sea Shore Middle School have incorporated strategies using the latest technology. Effective strategies and new developments in game fabrication are progressing, as more research is being conducted in this field. Technology, especially in AG, is being shaped by considering the needs and abilities of students (Lieberman & Donner, 2008), which might prove to be a valuable resource in the gymnasium.

A concerted effort by teachers to successfully include all students in physical education, regardless of their level of ability, could create a climate where all students progress in their motor skills (Lysniak, 2010). The modification of tasks to meet the needs of individual learners has been a concern for teachers, yet AG might inherently solve this issue. AG creates an environment where players' skill levels are matched with the gaming experience. This not only adds to the competence of the students but is also a very engaging tool for development of interest and skill (Roberts, 2001; Ryan & Deci, 2000).

Furthermore, students have a chance to practice the skills more frequently and over a longer period of time, if they, their friends, or family members own active games. AG is a new and promising frontier in the field of physical education and should be considered an option to augment more traditional ways of presenting activities in the gymnasia.

REFERENCES

Bernstein, E., Phillips, S. R., & Silverman, S. (2011). Attitudes and perceptions of middle school students toward competitive activities in physical education class. *Journal of Teaching in Physical Education, 30,* 69–83.

Carlson, T. B. (1995). We hate gym: Student alienation from physical education. *Journal of Teaching in Physical Education, 14,* 467–477.

Gibbone, A. (in press). Technology and instructional resources. In A. Lee (Ed.), *Moving and learning: Elementary physical education for the future.* Beijing, China: Higher Education Press.

Lieberman, D. A., & Donner, A. (2008). *Using electronic games to empower healthy lifestyles, prevention and self-care: Theory and research findings.* Retrieved from http://www.physicventures.com/news/using-electronic-games-empower-self-care

Lysniak, U. (2010). *Effective teaching strategies for low motor skill students.* (Doctoral Dissertation, Teachers College, Columbia University, 2010). Dissertation Abstracts International, AAT3424973.

Portman, P. A. (1995). Who is having fun in physical education classes? Experiences of sixth grade students in elementary and middle schools [Monograph]. *Journal of Teaching in Physical Education, 14,* 445–453.

Roberts, G. C. (2001). *Advances in motivation in sport and exercise.* Champaign, IL: Human Kinetics.

Ryan, R. M., & Deci, E. L. (2000). Self-determination theory and facilitation of intrinsic motivation, social development and well-being. *American Psychologist, 55,* 68–78.

Saslow, L. (2009, January 8). Moving from team sport to lifelong fitness. *New York Times.* Retrieved from http://www.nytimes.com/2009/01/11/nyregion/long-island/11gymli.html

Chapter Thirteen

Low SES Primary School Students Engaging in School Robotics Program

Vinesh Chandra, Annette Woods, and Amanda Levido

Recent attention in education within many western contexts has focused on improved outcomes for students, with a particular emphasis on closing the gap between those who come from disadvantaged backgrounds and the rest of the student population. Much of this attention has supported a set of simplistic solutions to improving scores on high-stakes standardized tests. The *collateral damage* (Nichols & Berliner, 2007) of such responses includes a narrowing of the curriculum, hitting plateaus in gain scores on the tests, and engaging in unproductive blame games aimed by the media and politicians at teachers and communities (Nichols & Berliner, 2007; Snyder, 2008).

Alternative approaches to improving the quality and equity of schooling remain as viable options to these unproductive measures. As an example in a recent study of school literacy reform in low SES (socioeconomic status) schools, Luke, Woods, and Dooley (2011) argued for the increase of substantive content and intellectual quality of the curriculum as a necessary means to re-engaging middle school students, improving outcomes of schooling, and achieving a high quality, high equity system.

The *MediaClub* is an after-school program for students in years four to seven (9- to 13-year-olds) at a primary school in a low SES area of a large Australian city. It is run as part of an Australian Research Council funded project. The aim of the program has been to provide an opportunity for students to gain expertise in digital technologies and media literacies in an after-school setting. It was hypothesized that the expertise students gain might then be used to shift the ways of being literate within classroom teaching and learning events.

Each term, there is a different focus on digital media, and information and communication technology (ICT) activities in the MediaClub. The work detailed in this chapter relates to a robotics program presented as one of the modules within this after-school setting. As part of the program, the participants were challenged to find creative solutions to problems in a constructivist learning environment.

MEDIACLUB: AN INNOVATIVE AFTER-SCHOOL PROGRAM

Outside school programs such as the MediaClub offer students an opportunity to engage with substantial content and skills in less formal learning contexts. These programs generally aim to offer young people a different learning environment from the one provided by the everyday classroom. Over recent years, engagement with technology-rich programs has become a key focus of many after-school learning programs. Digital storytelling (De-Gennaro, 2008), video game production (Peppler & Kafai, 2007; Willett, 2007), and video production (Gainer & Fink, 2008) are examples of such programs.

Research into these programs has suggested that such spaces are effective because they allow young people freedom to express themselves (Soep, 2006) in a participatory fashion. Peppler and Kafai (2007) argued that as young people engaged with technology, they were able to show their understanding of, and critique, mass media in complex ways. Media clubs also offer a space for young people to explore technology with varying degrees of intensity or formality.

Ito et al. (2008) described three contexts for engagement within such spaces—hanging out, messing around, and geeking out. In each of these contexts, the level of participation depends on the students' level of engagement with a particular project. According to Ito et al. (2008), young people are able to direct their learning and make choices about what interests them in spaces that take these purposes into account.

The MediaClub takes a different content focus in each of the four school terms. As examples, young people have created music, movies, and digital animations. The innovation described here involves a project that engaged young people with robotics' challenges in an eight-week program. As with all MediaClub programs, participants attended sessions for two hours on one afternoon each week.

The program was facilitated by university researchers and teachers, and held in the school's computer laboratory. The facilitators worked with the young people in ways that attempted to break down the traditional teacher–student interactional patterns. The young people who attended were encouraged to consider themselves as other than students. However, as many of the researchers were recognizable as teachers, the extent to which we achieved this shift in interaction remains variable.

ROBOTICS: AN EFFECTIVE AFTER-SCHOOL OPTION

The rapid growth in digital technologies over the past decade has led to the development of user-friendly robots that have the potential to encourage participants to solve problems and work collaboratively. However, despite their reported usefulness and adaptability, robotics activities are not often integrated in primary classrooms (Williams, Ma, Prejean, Ford, & Lai, 2008). The inability of teachers to design suitable activities is generally considered as a limitation to the uptake of robotics. This suggests a need to explore ways in which robotics activities can be designed, developed, and implemented to benefit primary school students.

More than 10 years ago, the Extended-Service Schools (ESS) Initiative was launched in the U.S. to support 60 after-school programs in 20 communities (Grossman et al., 2002). A review showed that the program had a positive benefit on the participants' attitudes and their behavior—both at and outside school.

The authors of this review used a multimethod approach that involved site visits and interviews of key stakeholders—staff, students, parents, and key city officials. Among the range of programs offered, LEGO robotics activities were found to be very effective and beneficial. Grossman et al. (2002) attributed the success of robotics to its (a) appeal to the youth culture, (b) motivation and engagement value, (c) technical challenge factor, (d) social and problem solving development options, and (e) alignment with academic disciplines such as mathematics.

Similarly, the Computer Clubhouse was set up in Boston almost 20 years ago (Rusk, Resnick, & Cooke, 2009); its primary objective is to enable disadvantaged young people to harness their creative talents using technology platforms such as robotics. The focus of learning is on "construction rather than instruction" (p. 2). Papert (1991) proposed the idea of constructionism, which asserts two key foundations to deep learning.

First, individuals develop their knowledge as a result of their hands-on experiences—an idea extrapolated from Piaget's constructivist theory. Second, by constructing products which have a personal significance, the learning is assumed to be more meaningful (Rusk et al., 2009). Modeling with robots can play a significant role in solving real-world problems. They simplify the problem solving process because their use involves physical manipulations (Nersessian, 2009). The assumption is that the partnership between the hand and head transforms challenges from abstract into concrete entities which, in turn, simplifies problem solving (Sennett, 2009).

The young people who engaged in the MediaClub robotics program were challenged to find creative solutions to problems in a constructivist learning environment using LEGO NXT robots. The 15 participants aged between 9 and 13 worked in groups of 3 to 4 and were facilitated by an instructor. Each week a challenge was presented to the participants. Over time, the complexity of these challenges increased as the level of scaffolding from staff decreased. Apart from hands-on problem solving, the sessions also created numerous opportunities for collaborative learning and teamwork.

Upon the completion of their tasks, the participants demonstrated their solutions to the problems to the rest of the group, which created multiple opportunities for reflective feedback. De Bono's (1999) six hats were used as the framework for guiding the students with their thinking. Analysis of participants' reflection sheets, in-class observations, and student interviews suggested that the hands-on activities effectively engaged them in a fun and interesting learning environment. While solving the problems, the young people also had numerous opportunities to draw connections between the task and the real world, and to concepts across STEM disciplines.

CHALLENGING YOUNG PEOPLE WITH ROBOTICS

De Bono's (1999) six hats served as an effective framework to develop questions which targeted specific aspects of the activity; these were used at the end of each activity with students being required to reflect on their approach to problem solving.

- The white hat question—"What was this challenge about?"—gave an idea of whether the participants' understood what the task was or not.
- The green hat question—"Draw a diagram to show how you tackled this challenge"—enabled participants to demonstrate their idea pictorially supported with some text.
- The yellow and black hat questions—"You had an idea on how you could tackle the challenge. What was good about your idea?" and "What was something about your idea that did not work the way you had planned?"—enabled the participants to critically reflect on the successes and failures of their designs.
- The blue and red hat questions—"What did you learn from this challenge?" and "If you did this challenge again, how would you change your idea?"—were perhaps the most significant ones to foster critical thinking.

The worksheets completed by the participants showed that there was evidence of in-depth and meaningful thinking (see Figure 13.1).

Interviews with students in focus group activities shed even more light on the value of this initiative in the after-school program. An array of questions was asked to enable the students to reflect on their experiences. Noting the interaction of the students from the interviews revealed that students found

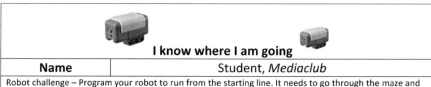

I know where I am going

Name	Student, *Mediaclub*

Robot challenge – Program your robot to run from the starting line. It needs to go through the maze and get back close to where it started. The robot must say "turn left" or "turn right" as it makes a turn.

What was this challenge about?
The challenge was about getting the robot to start at the black tape and travel through it [the maze] without crashing into a wall.

Draw a diagram to show how you tackled this challenge.

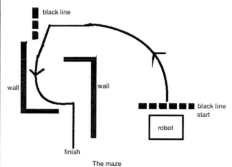

The maze   (Re-drawn from the student's sketch)

You had an idea on how you could tackle the challenge. What was good about your idea?
I think it was a good idea because I programmed it to go forwards without mistakes and the same for the backwards turn.

What was something about your idea that did not work the way you had planned?
We programmed the robot to do a 360 [degree turn] and also do a left-right turn. Also the duration was too much.

What did you learn from this challenge?
I learnt how to program the sensor and how to program the robot to go through the maze without bumping into anything. And to keep trying.

If you did this challenge again, how will you change your idea?
I will change my idea by changing directions it [the robot] was supposed to go in and put no curves to it.

Figure 13.1. Student Work Sample

robotics valuable for a range of reasons. Three key themes emerged from the analysis of these interviews: intrinsic motivation, cognitive development, and personal development.

Intrinsic Motivation

As reported in previous studies (see for example Grossman et al., 2002), intrinsic motivation has been a significant factor in drawing students from the school to the after-school robotics activities. The young people participating in the MediaClub robotics activity reported enjoying the experience because the activities *"were fun and were challenging."* There was an element of competition embedded in the activities and the students' recognition of this element was evident in their feedback.

While they were able to "play with robots," the increasing complexity of the challenges kept them engaged. As one group pointed out, "we've won every one, every challenge but we probably won't win this one." The young people also took the interview opportunity to record messages of appreciation to staff because this experience offered them new opportunities to learn. They reported that the after-school experiences were enjoyable and, as a consequence, they had "a great time on Thursday afternoons."

Cognitive Development

Cognitive development was another key theme that emerged from the feedback. The participants were developing their own strategies for problem solving. These strategies ranged from a logical approach focused on getting the angle and timing right to devising their own problem solving strategies. As one participant pointed out, they worked through the challenge "step by step and not all in one go because (it was) much easier to see how it (the robot) was going and running and what our progress was." For some students, a trial-and-error technique was one of the strategies that worked.

The activities also created other learning opportunities in which participants were able to see the connection between the challenges and the real world. They noted that "This is a life challenge that we're doing in Media-Club today." Comments such as "challenges were really stretching my mind to think creatively" suggest that participants were getting opportunities to engage in tasks that drew upon higher order thinking skills (Rusk et al., 2009).

While robotics enabled them to do the "cool stuff [which was] really awesome," there were times when it was too difficult. For example, they commented that whenever "we crashed into walls and stuff it would be really frustrating." The use of the word *we* in this explanation suggests that students were seeing the robot as part of their group. "The control of the robot is actually the person... if you're saying it wasn't working that means you're not working." This comment provides an insight into students' understanding of the function of human cognition in the workings of the robots. It suggests that the robot is a part of their team—if the team fails, so does the robot.

Personal Development

Personal development was another important concept that emerged from the data with a specific focus on teamwork. Sometimes the teams did not function as effectively as they could have. Given that these participants were from three different grade levels who would otherwise not meet during school hours, the challenges of forming, storming, norming, and performing as groups were expected (Tuckman, 1965).

As one student pointed out, she "had to change groups [because] my group wasn't paying attention to me and not listening to me." All students knew the importance of being able to work together to achieve desirable outcomes. One student elaborated on this by pointing out that "maybe we need to work on group work" before they started to address the challenges. They proposed ideas on how groups could function more effectively; for example, "maybe you could have less people in a group... maybe like two and not too many."

Participants acknowledged that they would take some of the experiences of robotics in the MediaClub back to their classrooms and share them with their classmates. This was like a *flow-on-effect:* what they had learned in the after-school program was not isolated but rather valuable to mainstream schooling. They believed that if robotics was embedded as a classroom activity, they would be able share their knowledge and "present what [they have] learnt this term in media club." Applying the experience of working in teams to classroom activities and elsewhere was also identified as a benefit of participating in the MediaClub.

CONCLUSION

The experiences of the students suggest that the MediaClub was more than just learning about robotics. It would seem that, in this environment, students were also learning about *learning*, thus developing metacognitive skills. In addition, they benefitted from learning how to work together to solve challenging problems linked to substantive issues and content (Luke et al., 2011).

Intrinsic motivation in this after-school program was driven by enjoyment and the engaging nature of the robotics activities. The challenging and competitive nature of the open-ended tasks led participants to develop their own strategies for problem solving. The tasks presented a range of opportunities for learning and personal development as the participants found strategies that supported teamwork. The experiences of the young people in the Media-Club demonstrate that activities such as robotics have the potential to engage participants effectively in learning environments. In doing so, such activities enhance the intellectual quality of the programs that are offered to young people.

ACKNOWLEDGMENTS

We extend our thanks to the teachers and administrators who are our research partners on this project and we acknowledge the partnership of the Queensland Teachers Union and the support of the Australian Research Council. Our colleagues on the project are: Allan Luke, Karen Dooley, Michael Dezuanni, Amanda Levido, Katherine Doyle, Beryl Exley, John Davis, and Kathy Mills of Queensland University of Technology, and John McCollow and Lesley McFarlane of the Queensland Teachers Union.

REFERENCES

De Bono, E. (1999). *Six thinking hats*. New York, NY: Back Bay Books.

DeGennaro, D. (2008). The dialectics informing identity in an urban youth digital storytelling workshop. *E-learning, 5*, 420–444.

Gainer, J., & Fink, L. S. (2008). Who is DeAndre? Tapping the power of popular culture in literacy learning. *Voices from the Middle, 16*(1), 23–30.

Grossman, J. B., Price, M. L., Fellerath, V., Jucovy, L., Kotloff, L., Raley, R., & Walker, K. (2002). *Multiple choices after school: Findings from the Extended-Service Schools initiative*. Retrieved from http://www.mdrc.org/publications/48/full.pdf

Ito, M., Horst, H., Bittanti, M., Boyd, D., Herr-Stephanson, B., Lange, P., et al. (2008). *Living and learning with new media: Summary of findings from the Digital Youth Project*. Cambridge, MA: The MIT Press.

Luke, A., Woods, A., & Dooley, K. (2011). Comprehension as social and intellectual practice: Rebuilding curriculum in low socioeconomic and cultural minority schools.*Theory into Practice, 50*, 157–164.

Nersessian, N. J. (2009). How do engineering scientists think? Model-based simulation in biomedical engineering research laboratories. *Topics in Cognitive Science, 1*, 730–757.

Nichols, S., & Berliner, D. (2007). *Collateral damage: How high-stakes testing corrupts America's schools*. Cambridge, MA: Harvard Education Press.

Papert, S. (1991). Situating constructionism. In S. Papert & I. Harel (Eds.), *Constructionism* (pp. 1–11). Norwood, NJ: Ablex.

Peppler, K. A., & Kafai, Y. B. (2007). From SuperGoo to Scratch: Exploring creative digital media production in informal learning. *Media and Technology, 32*, 149–166.

Rusk, N., Resnick, M., & Cooke, S. (2009). Origins and guiding principles of the Computer Clubhouse. In Y. B. Kafai, K. A. Peppler, & R. N. Chapman. (Eds.), *The computer clubhouse: Constructionism and creativity in youth communities* (pp. 17–25). New York, NY: Teachers College Press.

Sennett, R. (2009). *The craftsman*. London, United Kingdom: Penguin.

Snyder, I. (2008). *The literacy wars: Why teaching children to read and write is a battleground in Australia*. Sydney, Australia: Allen & Unwin.

Soep, E. (2006). Beyond literacy and voice in youth media production. *McGill Journal of Education, 41*, 197–213.

Tuckman, B. W. (1965). Developmental sequence in small groups. *Psychological Bulletin, 16,* 249–272.

Willett, R. (2007). Technology, pedagogy and digital production: A case study of children learning new media skills. *Learning Media and Technology, 32,* 167–181.

Williams, D. C., Ma, Y., Prejean, L., Ford, M. J., & Lai, G. (2008). Acquisition of physics content knowledge and scientific inquiry skills in a robotics summer camp. *Journal of Research on Technology in Education, 40,* 201–216.

Chapter Fourteen

Stepping into Pictures and Music Scores: Imaginative Dramatic Play

Joanne Kilgour Dowdy and Mary T. Toepfer

"It is unthinkable to Mrs. Biswell that such a mediocre-to-poor student could actually like school, so she concludes that his antics and reckless enthusiasms are merely ploys to annoy her" (Spinelli, 2002, p. 55).

READING ADOLESCENTS

In the young adult novel *Loser* (Spinelli, 2002), the narrator describes a scene in which the protagonist reacts in a completely unexpected way to the taunts of another student who is older and bolder than he is. The narrator explains that this unusual reaction—a smile instead of a frown or scream of annoyance—"has just cheated the boy" (p. 23), because he was counting on making his victim, Zinkoff, cry. Instead, Zinkoff "sends his best smile up to join the one above" (p. 23) that is being displayed by the taller boy who took Zinkoff's hat.

This is only one incident in a series of scenes where the young Zinkoff, the so-called loser, does not interpret correctly the body language of those around him. He gets into trouble on more than one occasion because he examines others and receives different messages than the others intend for him to understand. The way that people talk and physicalize their expression when they communicate seems foreign to him. The necessary, and often lifesaving, skill that allows us to read people and understand the contexts in which they express their choices is one source of expertise that young people usually carry into classrooms; therefore, teachers should consider how to use this valuable tool in the service of formal literacy instruction.

ARTS-BASED LITERACY INSTRUCTION

What counts as literacy often seems political in nature, as poetry, music, visual art, videos, or dramatic presentations are all included in the canon of artistic expressions available to literacy teachers. PK–12 learners enhance their thinking, learn more perspectives, and become better readers, writers, and speakers when they create or study products in an arts-based classroom (Albers, 2001).

Rinaldo, Erwin, and Phillips (2008), for example, reported that an arts-based curriculum significantly contributed to the improved writing scores of at-risk students. They made the case that engaged students are far more likely to be productive in classrooms and that the arts are one means to gain the students' attention and maintain it for developing formal literacy.

Other researchers concur with the perspective that the arts stimulate learning since they found that students who merely study from textbooks and take standardized tests are not as successful as those who are exposed to the arts (Otten, Stigher, Woodward, & Staley, 2004). Much like the findings of Kist (2002, 2005) and Bruce (2004, 2008), proponents of arts-based instruction report that some students attain a new level of fluency in their exchange of ideas with others. Gallagher and Ntelioglou (2011) found drama, specifically, to be able to accomplish this new level, stating that drama has the ability to improve the relationship between the multiple ways of making sense of what we learn and the many ways of expressing our understanding of these insights.

FRAMEWORK FOR READING AND WRITING IN ADOLESCENCE AND ADULTHOOD

A course designed to teach reading and writing methods to enhance success with adolescents and adults uses a workshop approach to introduce teacher candidates to poetry, film analysis and composition, critical literacy, drama, visual art, and music interpretation as a prompt for creative writing. The preservice teachers learn of the many literacy practices and needs that adolescents have in their lives; literacy within school that is used for nonacademic purposes (Finders, 1997), then, is brought into the classroom for academic purposes, and the preservice teachers design lessons to meet the needs of their adolescent students.

In the workshops, teacher candidates are led through a series of steps that help them experience the process of creating a product in a particular genre. They might use poetry as a means to develop a storyboard, create a character's costume based on the information from the attitude that is garnered from a scene offered in a novel, or step into a painting or music score—the latter of which comprises the sections that follow.

These preservice teachers typically raise questions about the challenges that they might expect in their own classrooms. They consider issues of gathering materials like art supplies, or convincing the principal of an alternative school that showing a film in class is not a way to avoid serious work. The class as a whole then brainstorms ideas about integrating the arts workshops into lesson plans that meet the standards for various content areas. Teacher candidates are reminded that doing a draft of a lesson plan is not an examination, a task that is right or wrong based on an outsider's grading rubric, but a process that would lead to a final product.

Most important, it is the social justice aspect of the teacher preparation agenda that the workshops seek to address. By tending to the sociocultural dimensions of literacy, teacher educators are able to facilitate the student teachers' recognition of the need to make connections to students' lives and to the world outside of school. Taking on different perspectives in a situation, learning to negotiate multimodal forms of communication, and reading the behaviors of others all provide the teachers with practical experience in communicating each content area's syllabus from a multitude of entry points.

THE WORKSHOP: INTO THE PICTURE

Workshop participants learn how to step into musical scores by first stepping into paintings. The point, as Gallagher and Ntelioglou (2011) explained, is that "Using drama or role-playing makes it possible for students to step back and examine the motives and the psychology of characters in their story" (p. 329). With that worthwhile endeavor in mind, teachers might facilitate a group to enter a picture and bring it to life through the following drama techniques:

1. Present an image to participants from which they will select a character.
2. Highlight the variety of characters that participants can select from the image shown, offering them people, items, and colors in the image as viable candidates.
3. Each participant chooses one of the characters in the image and creates a character story for that individual or object (Who am I? Where am I? What is my story?)
4. In groups, the participants decide how to represent the image in which their character exists, as a tableau, with each participant taking on a role inside of the image and bringing the image to life. This means that

even certain items or colors in the image will be portrayed by someone, not just the people in the image.

5. The class will look at each group's tableau of the image.
6. Each person in a group will create a character sketch for his or her
   chosen character in the picture. Answering questions—Who am I?
   What is happening in this picture? When is this taking place? Where is
   this taking place? and Why do I feel the way I do?—will help each
   participant to write a first-person narrative about the character that he
   or she selects from the picture. In doing so, participants can (a) decide
   on a crisis event or a discovery that their character experiences in the
   course of his or her life. For example, if the character has had a parent
   die, details about this critical event would create a better understanding of what this character has endured; (b) discuss in the narrative how
   the character used the crisis event or discovery to resolve new challenges that have since evolved in the character's life; (c) select a
   character sketch—from a comic book, graphic novel, newspaper comic strip, or children's coloring book—in order to provide a face that
   matches the person whom they have created in their narrative. Such
   creative writing activities work in conjunction with each other to provide a complete character sketch, making the character believable and
   ready to be shared.
7. Share each person's character sketch in the group.
8. Taking places in the tableau again, the characters will answer two
   questions when the teacher touches them on the shoulder: Who are
   you? and What are you doing here? The characters answer based on
   the narrative that they have created.
9. Discuss in each group the actual events that led up to the situation that
   the image captures. Determine a beginning, middle, and end to the
   scene that will begin when the tableau comes to life. Each character
   should have something to say, or a reaction, when the scene is presented for the rest of the class.
10. Review the process of arriving at the scene that was created for the
    group in the tableau: What writing steps did the group follow? How
    does this process support literacy development?

The tableau enables participants to create collaboratively as they bring the
image to life. In addition, because they have written the narrative ahead of
time about the chosen character that they are representing, participants can be
spontaneous about sharing the story that leads them to the point in their lives
where onlookers meet them in the frozen scene. The story, then, creates a
foundation from which participants can draw and ensures that all the participants in a group ask each character in the scene about his or her purpose for
being in the scene.

Through the tableau, participants have a chance to use their imagination within the context of the story that the group is representing. Those who are watching the tableau come to life are learning as well, because they see the story grammar unfold—the beginning, middle, and end of the character's narrative—as a function of what happens when we dare to imagine.

MUSIC NOTES BECOME CHARACTERS

Another level of daring to imagine takes place in a workshop in which music scores are used, like those by J. Rosamund Johnson, George Harrison, Claude-Michel Schonberg, Arthur Herzog and Billie Holiday, and Keith Christopher. Workshop participants work together in small groups to examine the musical notes on the pages of the score in an effort to find patterns that seem to communicate a message.

For example, if they seem to see several bold notes in a row, representing loud discharges of sound, perhaps the notes are characters who are shouting something angrily. Or if the notes are shown as low, soft sounds, the message becomes one of a peaceful nature. Participants begin to see the notes as symbols that are able to deliver more information than merely the tune they collectively dictate. The symbols become the characters *on stage* with a story to tell, permitting participants to take their music score and treat it as a narrative with a beginning, middle, and end.

After doing the above, one particular group in a workshop shared a story about being crowded into a place of residence. They came to such a conclusion upon seeing in their music score that there were many small symbols standing alongside each other in only a few areas while the majority of the page consisted of blank areas where notes should have been. This phenomenon represented for them a tight environment, such as a tiny apartment.

Subsequently, they created a story about a relationship that might exist in the long line of single notes, deciding that such notes were frustrated figures who lined up one after another on the page, squeezing into their constricted space. The characters saw the spacious, blank areas on their page and yearned to break free from their uniform, claustrophobic line that oppressed them. In an effort to overcome this stress due to the structure of their immediate environment, two participants, in a tableau, displayed one person trying to get away from the other.

When tapped by the instructor, they spoke a dialogue that represented an intense argument in which one was explaining her need to escape while the other was insisting that during the conversation, she should remain in place. To complement this interchange, the actors used tightened fists and other physical actions that evidenced a conflict. When asked to freeze, the heightened facial expressions and body language took the original tableau to a new level.

The premise for using the musical notes is that an improvisational dialogue evolves. Participants respond to each other in a back-and-forth exchange as musical notes would typically respond if representing a certain human attitude. Although participants sometimes find it challenging to maintain the attitude that they have been presenting, they must continue to be bossy or angry or impatient in order to keep a conversation going with another character. *Breaking character* abruptly halts the conversation.

If they can perpetuate the different body movements and voices that they normally do not use in a conversation, performers will successfully advance the dialogue as well as establish a mood. Such a process becomes a satisfying learning experience, not only for those involved in the action but also for those outside of the dialogue as well.

DISCUSSION

When learners step into images or become musical notes, teachers allow them to use what they know in order to take them to the unknown. Enhancing student confidence in the ability to make sense of the world and to apply such an understanding to academic achievement is important (Hilliard, as cited in Dowdy & Wynne, 2005). When learners experience success, they are more willing to take risks in how they learn.

The high performing schools that Langer (2001) described all demonstrate that "active and engaged students and teachers" were members of an "effective learning environment" (p. 856) where students could think, using English as a means for accomplishing tasks. The motivation that is achieved through these positive experiences acts as scaffolding for other learning interests and demonstrates to the students that they are capable of creating knowledge that is useful.

Celebrating students' accomplishments, one teacher described her observations at the end of a workshop in the following way:

> We are the class who . . . dances, sings, acts/does dramas, reads books about how to teach drama with our students, has talk shows, listens, puts ourselves into character, laughs, overcomes anxiety, learns from doing, has snacks (this is all from one class—bravo!).

This reflection demonstrates the rationale that Wilhelm and Edmiston (1998) gave for using drama in the classroom. According to them, "drama encourages all students' participation because it is so inclusive. . . . Students who find reading and writing barriers to comprehension and communication are not excluded" (p. 113).

When student expertise in reading body language is used as a bridge to enhancing other forms of visual literacy skills through drama, teachers are helping to develop a critical literacy stance to learning and meaning making. Students become confident about looking inward for self-definition; gain expertise in learning how to use their own experience in order to imagine the lived reality of others; and, most important, take the knowledge from various experiences and observations and interact with the world using an informed and intellectually curious stance.

Taking a cue from the adolescent Astrid Magnussen in *White Oleander* (Fitch, 1999), teachers can come to rely on the ability of youth to know and believe in themselves. As she confronts two college girls who have come to meet her in an effort to show solidarity with her imprisoned mother, Magnussen says of herself:

> Suddenly, I became aware of what I must seem like to them. Hard, street. My eyeliner, my black polyester shirt, my heavy black boots, my cascade of silver earrings, hoops from pinkie-sized to softball. Niki and Yvonne had pierced my ears one day when they were bored. I let them do it. It pleased them to shape me. I'd learned, whatever you hung from my earlobes or put on my back, I was insoluble, like sand in water. Stir me up, I always came to rest on the bottom. (Fitch, 1999, p. 322)

In truth, if teachers listened to young people explain what they must appear to be like in the eyes of adults, such teachers could develop new perspectives from the youths' understanding of themselves and others. Thanks to the arts, the door to listening can be opened.

REFERENCES

Albers, P. (2001). Literacy in the arts. *Primary Voices K-6, 9*(4), 3–9.

Bruce, D. L. (2004). Visualizing success: Using video composition in the classroom. *Ohio Journal of English Language Arts, 44*(1), 51–56.

Bruce, D. L. (2008). Visualizing literacy: Building bridges with media. *Reading & Writing Quarterly, 24*, 264–282.

Dowdy, J. K., & Wynne, J. (Eds.). (2005). *Racism, research, and educational reform: Voices from the city.* New York, NY: Peter Lang.

Finders, M. J. (1997). *Just girls: Hidden literacies and life in junior high.* New York, NY: Teachers College Press.

Fitch, J. (1999). *White oleander: A novel.* New York, NY: Little, Brown and Company.

Gallagher, K., & Ntelioglou, B. Y. (2011). Which new literacies? Dialogue and performance in youth writing. *Journal of Adolescent and Adult Literacy, 54*, 322–330.

Kist, W. (2002). Finding "new literacy" in action: An interdisciplinary high school western civilization class. *Journal of Adolescent & Adult Literacy, 45*, 368–377.

Kist, W. (2005). *New literacies in action: Teaching and learning in multiple media.* New York, NY: Teachers College Press.

Langer, J. A. (2001). Beating the odds: Teaching middle and high school students to read and write well. *American Educational Research Journal, 38*, 837–880. Retrieved from http://www.jstor.org/pss/3202505

Otten, M., Stigher, J., Woodward, J. A., & Staley, L. (2004). Performing history: The effects of a dramatic art-based history program on student achievement and enjoyment. *Theory and Research in Social Education, 32*, 187–212.

Rinaldo, V., Erwin, R., & Phillips, D. K. (2008). *Improving the writing scores of at-risk students through arts-based instruction.* Retrieved from http://www.learnercentereded.org/jpact/Articles/Spring2009/Rinaldo.pdf

Spinelli, J. (2002). *Loser.* New York, NY: Scholastic.

Wilhelm, J. D., & Edmiston, B. (1998). *Imagining to learn: Inquiry, ethics, and integration through drama.* Portsmouth, NH: Heinemann.

Chapter Fifteen

Classrooms or Rock Stages? Learning Music Through Collaboration

Rut Martínez-Borda, Pilar Lacasa, María Ruth García-Pernía, and Sara Cortés-Gómez

VIDEO GAMES IN HIGH SCHOOL

Recently, an entire high school decided to introduce commercial video games into the classroom to use along with textbooks, movies, cameras, and traditional blackboards. To explore the educational power of these new means, a team of specialists in education and technology—the Culture, Technology, and New Literacies Research Group from the University of Alcalá, Spain—worked together with the teachers. This chapter discusses the innovative experiences led by Ms. García, the music teacher, and her group of 15-year-old students. One of the researchers' impressions after the first session was as follows:

> We went to the music classroom, which turned out to be a great choice. The class is really appropriate, full of musical instruments. I had the feeling that it was not a classroom . . . the key was that it did not feel like a classroom, but rather like an informal learning environment.

Covering the mandated curriculum is a significant concern among teachers, but the content knowledge that should be acquired does not always motivate the students. If, in the past, movies, television, and newspapers were relevant forms of authentic media to motivate students, today video games might play a similar role. To this end, the goal of the participating teachers and researchers was to identify innovative educational practices whenever commercial video games—particularly the music-oriented game "Rock Band"—were utilized in a secondary classroom. These approaches are designed to develop new media literacies within collaborative learning contexts that also incorporate other new or traditional technologies (Lacasa, Martínez-Borda, & Méndez, 2008).

In Ms. García's classroom, the teacher and researchers discovered how video games can be educational when combined with other tools. This contributed not only to the motivation of students, to the engagement in the learning process, and to the transformation of the classroom, but also impacted the development of learners as literate persons (Lacasa, Martínez-Borda, & Méndez, 2009). Our intent is to describe this innovative practice by demonstrating how commercial video games may promote motivation to learn, as well as develop creative thinking, while new knowledge is constructed in the secondary school context.

Why Bring Video Games Into the Classroom?

During their first interview, Ms. García, the music teacher, and the researchers who worked with her raised many questions about video games and why educators should work with them:

- What can they teach us?
- How do we use them in the classroom?
- What is the role of music in a video game?
- Do we make teenagers aware of the power of musical art?
- Can we teach music to high school students so that they find it useful and motivating?
- Do students know how to use music as a language?

Through our exploration of these questions, we concluded that video games represent one of the most significant *cultural emergent forms* present in children's leisure time between the ages of 8 and 18 (Livingstone, 2002). In that sense, games are generating a new communication scenario in which the classic elements of communication are transformed. Players share not only a form of leisure and a technological skill, but also the experience of exploring a different symbolic universe, by submersing themselves in a multimedia and virtual world.

As an outcome, educators are slowly discovering new reasons to use video games, since these tools allow them to approach situations that are part of the daily life of teenagers. To describe this experience, we need to understand—both from theoretical and practical points of view—what video games are and what purpose they serve. In this chapter, we are focusing particularly on games that involve music in order to better understand their potential for educational purposes.

UNDERSTANDING VIDEO GAMES

Gee's (2003) and Jenkins's (2006) work provided the theoretical framework for our innovation and research questions. They noted that commercial video games are designed for leisure and entertainment, but they can also be used as powerful educational tools. Although there are multiple ways of using video games educationally, the ones that are more closely related to our goals are as follows:

- *Using video games as a vehicle for curriculum attainment:* To replace traditional forms of media (such as cinema and television), video games can help motivate students to master the grade-appropriate curriculum.
- *Acquiring new "languages" and ways of thinking:* Video games conceal a hidden curriculum from which one can learn (Gee & Hayes, 2010). Their inherent capacity to simulate reality is a first step towards understanding complex problems.
- *Combining video games with other technologies:* Information and communication technologies are not usually mutually exclusive. The combined presence of other tools allows us to communicate and express ourselves through multiple languages (Jenkins, 2006)—not just through written communication but also through audiovisual discourse.

Musical Video Games as Instructional Tools

Human beings have many different ways of expressing themselves, including the language of music. What roles may music-oriented video games play when it comes to learning or teaching music as a language? Ms. García realized that music-oriented games such as *Rock Band* offer the opportunity for making music in a simple yet engaging way. Players create a band and emulate their favorite musicians within a virtual world.

The challenge of *Rock Band* (a very popular video game created in 2007) is for players to maintain the rhythm of a song by accompanying it with an instrument. Most music-oriented games include a wide variety of simulation controllers (such as drums, guitars, and microphones); these peripherals allow players to sing and play an instrument to the rhythm of the music. Each player's skill level is scored on the musical notes produced, all of which is reflected on the game screen. In our quest to introduce this innovative tool in the music classroom, we wanted to know how music video games contribute to the educational process. We anticipated the following:

- *Music motivates and moves: Rock Band* allows for the teaching and learning of music to become a living process. Sounds are part of a concert that arises from personal experiences mixed in a collective production.

Thoughts and reflections are not the only elements to teach curriculum contents in education; *Rock Band* may contribute to channeling students' emotions as well (Salen & Zimmerman, 2005).

- *Working together is more important than competing:* In a video game, real and virtual worlds intertwine through actions that turn individuals into a band requiring rapport, collaboration, and teamwork in order to make music (Knobel & Lankshear, 2010). Students can write the lyrics of their songs and express their own ideas and feelings.

THE CLASSROOM AS A MULTIMODAL SETTING

During Ms. García's class, every student was given multiple opportunities to play *Rock Band* and enjoyed the possibility of continuously living between the real and the virtual world. However, the introduction of this game into the classroom contributed not only to the participants' feeling the power of music in a virtual world, but also to transforming the classroom's physical space and the relationship among the participants.

Classroom or Rock Stage?

One of the first outcomes Ms. García and the researchers observed was that the classroom changed: the furniture was removed to create the "stage" and to enable more interaction among musicians and their audience. One of the researchers reflected,

> They start to play. It´s a different classroom. Real-virtual instruments are introduced. There are no small groups, they all play in one group with both real and virtual instruments. Several singers, a choir, dancers, real instruments (coconuts, bongos, drums, cymbals, tambourine) and virtual instruments. The tables are not spread out: there is only a "stage," the place where the group is going to perform. Students, teacher and researchers come together, dance, play, and act. It's hard to say who is who.

By using both virtual and real instruments, Ms. García and the researchers transformed the teaching–learning setting. The fact of living between two worlds—the real one (the music classroom) and the virtual one (the Rock Band)—allowed students to discover and experience new sensations. But how did we move from one scenario to the other? The process was progressive and the key was to play several sessions of the game. One day, the teacher challenged her students even further by asking them to use real instruments along with the virtual ones: A Spanish guitar, tambourines, drums, and other instruments were enthusiastically taken off the shelves.

The usual classroom furniture was put aside to encourage movement and interaction between the musicians and the audience who cheered them on during the performance. Subsequently, the behavior in the classroom was transformed. With these two elements, the classroom had become an informal environment where, for example, the audience applauded and cheered their classmates as if they were real fans in a concert.

The transformational moment, however, came when some students continued with the virtual instruments shown on the video screen, while the rest of the class started improvising with tambourines, drums, electric and Spanish guitars, cymbals, and so on. This kind of music making generated a distinct atmosphere, not just due to student collaboration, but as a result of the spontaneity of the music and the creation of new versions of familiar songs as well.

The Class as a Music Band: The Value of the Team

In addition to meeting curricular goals, the use of music-oriented video games can also contribute to the classroom through the transformation of social relationships, especially among students. Video games—more than any other types of games—help foster collaboration among peers through the availability of the multi-player mode.

The teacher and the researchers showed students the possibilities that the game offered while they talked and played along with them. Overcoming the difficulties of the virtual musical world became easier together because the video game offered the possibility to rescue teammates and help players rejoin the game. Working as a team became more important than ever before in Ms. García's class.

In the real world, members of music bands rehearse for hours in order for everyone to play the same rhythm. In the virtual world, the situation is not very different since students are challenged to play as one. For example, the singer of the band remarked, "I don´t know how to, I´ve tried, and we have failed miserably, both with the guitar and the drums." Within this context, playing in a music band means playing to the best of one's ability so that the result is success for the group.

As a music teacher, Ms. García understands this process and its value, making this one of the goals of her teaching. In addition, the students learned that it is important for classmates to show support for each other, in an effort not to be eliminated from the game. A student noted, "I think it´s better to play in groups because this way we all practice a little."

The Teacher as an Agent of Change

Introducing commercial video games into the classroom directly influenced the role of the teacher. In formal contexts, the distance between the adult and the student is usually quite significant, but Ms. García's introduction of media that is present in the out-of-school lives of teenagers in the classroom allowed for the reduction of this distance. Students tend to be experts in the use of new technologies and the teaching–learning process becomes collaborative, with everyone learning from everyone else, as depicted in Figure 15.1.

In the workshop, capitalizing on student expertise and engagement contributed to the transformation of the classroom. The researcher (an expert in the video game) helped teenagers several times so they could become familiar with the virtual instruments. Comparatively, Ms. García offered support for her students at all times, aiding them in the process of making music. From the first session, the teacher became the driving force behind the transformation of the learning experience—she encouraged the students, applauded them, danced to the music, and helped them manage the songs by setting the pace.

Ms. García became integrated as any other member in a rock band. Her disposition helped students become uninhibited and encouraged their active participation in the workshop. During the process, Ms. García adopted a range of different roles; as the moment demanded, she acted as a teacher, journalist, musical artist, audience member, and so on. Her success with her students throughout the sessions was her power to consistently motivate.

Figure 15.1. Ms. García engages her students

Photographer: María Ruth García Pernía

MUSIC VIDEO GAMES AS A WAY TO LEARN DIFFERENTLY

Ms. García and the collaborating researchers showed the importance of making music and how students understand music as a language. In this sense, we have seen how music-oriented video games reveal themselves as a possible tool for classroom learning, mostly because students learned to work as a group. In a band, everyone has an individual role, but it becomes important for all members to work together for the final outcome to be successful.

Additionally, the presence of music-oriented video games in the classroom contributed to transforming the relationship between Ms. García and her students, which became much closer and more reciprocal. Finally, the classroom became an informal learning environment: the furniture was removed to create the stage and to enable interaction between the musicians and their audience. This, together with the merging of virtual and real instruments, transformed the teaching–learning setting.

REFERENCES

Gee, J. P. (2003). *What video games have to teach us about learning and literacy.* New York, NY: Palgrave Macmillan.

Gee, J. P., & Hayes, E. R. (2010). *Women and gaming: The Sims and 21st century learning.* New York, NY: Palgrave Macmillan.

Jenkins, H. (2006). *Convergence culture: Where old and new media collide.* New York, NY: New York University Press.

Knobel, M., & Lankshear, C. (2010). *DIY Media: Creating, sharing and learning with new technologies*. New York, NY: Peter Lang.

Lacasa, P., Martínez-Borda, R., & Méndez, L. (2008). Bringing commercial games into the classrooms. *Computers and Composition, 25*, 331-358.

Lacasa, P., Martínez-Borda, R., & Méndez, L. (2009). Learning how to use videogames as educational tools: Building bridges between commercial and serious games. In M. Mankaanranta & P. Neittaanmäki (Eds.), *Design and use of serious games* (pp. 107-126). Dordrecht, the Netherlands: Springer Science + Business Media B.V.

Livingstone, S. (2002). *Young people and new media.* London, UK: Sage.

Salen, K., & Zimmerman, E. (2005). Game design and meaningful play. In J. Raessens & J. Goldstein (Eds.), *Handbook of computer games studies* (pp. 59-79). Cambridge, MA: The MIT Press.

IV

Connecting School Culture, Community, and Student Success

On any given day, in one professor's mailbox are journals with broad themes focused on leading for change, supporting students' academic growth and getting results, motivating teachers and learners, as well as engaging parents and colleagues. In a nearby principal's in-box, there are directives and memos, statements from the superintendent, readings on how to involve the school board and community, as well as suggestions on how to attain 21st century schools.

Similarly, teachers' mailboxes are chock full of mandates, the latest strategies, shortcuts to learning, and standards. Are the constructs for researchers, administrators, and teachers mutually exclusive? Or, are there *overarching* themes that can support new teachers, master teachers, educational leaders, professors, community members, and policy makers?

In editing this book, we frequently found the theme of student engagement to be at the core of the chapters, thus becoming an overarching theme and key construct that may lead to school improvement. We were inspired by Blankstein's (2007) message that there is a *need to reengage*:

> Clearly, if students are bored, they are also disengaged; for them, success in school is an uphill struggle. Likewise, teachers and administrators who feel overwhelmed, burdened with educational mandates, or whipsawed by a string of change initiatives that lacked the buy-in to succeed will also be prone to disengage. By contrast, schools that have fully engaged their stakeholders create collective energy toward continuous improvement. (p. 22)

This section of the book offers documentary accounts of successful initiatives that have been created from hard-won wisdom and *create collective energy*; innovative programs created by teachers, administrators, and researchers who recognize that change is needed to support the ideal of quality education for every learner. The practical wisdom offered here is a reminder that student motivation and engagement are the basis of successful schools.

In the first chapter of this section by Judy W. Yu, readers are introduced to a Chinese American after-school program that highlights the urgent need for school administrators, educators, and community-based organizations to collaborate and develop culturally relevant teaching practices and a critical multicultural curriculum that is reflective of the ethnic American history and lives of all students.

David Zyngier offers a detailed account of an innovative project that partnered university and community volunteers with schools where student learning difficulties and disengagement are significant issues. *Students of promise* were at the center of the alternative program in Australia as they benefited from an opportunity to experience greater community engagement. In an examination of secondary Montessori schools, Wendy J. LaRue and Peter Hoffman-Kipp describe a give-and-take learning environment in which teachers and students are learning and succeeding together.

The theme of service-learning is introduced by Lane Perry, Billy O'Steen, and Peter Cammock as they examine how student engagement is influenced in a positive way in New Zealand. In one key aspect, the *active-learning* theme—based on the students' experiences—represents the opportunity to learn from doing (*ma te mahi e ako ai*), as well as applying what is learned from total life experiences. Last but not least, Della R. Leavitt and Erin N. Washington share an uplifting example of a teacher who is not only an expert in her content area, but truly believes all her students can succeed, personifies integrity, and supports student empowerment in the mathematics classroom and beyond.

The innovations and compelling narratives documented in this book, and particularly in this section, are often the results of trial and error, hard-won wisdom, and a common belief that teachers can persevere and successfully meet the needs of all students.

REFERENCE

Blankstein, A. M. (2007). Terms of engagement: Where failure is not an option. In A. M. Blankstein, R. W. Cole, & P. D. Houston (Eds.). *Engaging every learner* (pp. 1–28). Thousand Oaks, CA: Corwin Press.

Chapter Sixteen

Growing Up Chinese American

Judy W. Yu

Voices of children chanting "ching-chong" resonate in Minsi Chung's mind as their stinging chimes have become imprints of her own school memories. Since the age of five, she has witnessed and experienced the repercussions of systemic inequities based on her race, class, linguistic accents, and citizenship status in public school. On the streets of New York City, Minsi and her Asian friends were victimized and assaulted for being "chinks" and in high school, teachers omitted the history of Asian American pioneers from their lesson plans because it was said that "we just can't study everybody."

Growing up as a Chinese immigrant, Minsi's construction of knowledge has been enriched by her experiences in an urban context. Minsi was born in Guangzhou, China, and immigrated to the United States when she was eight years old. Now at age 16, Minsi lives in a small, cramped apartment in Chinatown with her parents and older sister. Her father is a cook in a Chinese restaurant in Chinatown, and her mother is a dishwasher. Minsi's parents work 12 to 14 hours a day. She does not get an opportunity to spend much time with her parents; however, watching them work reminds Minsi of the daily struggle of immigrant life and the importance of obtaining a good education.

In a working class immigrant family, Minsi paid homage to schools and entrusted teachers to *educate* her in fulfilling her greatest scholastic potential. However, Minsi's trust in schools and teachers dissipated when she began to experience an academic and personal dissonance in her education. As Minsi grew older, her personal experiences at home and her academic experiences in school erupted with tensions of inequalities. She was conflicted about her education, the presentation of school curricula, and her teachers' practices as she did not see nor learn about herself, her culture, her community, and the diversity of people that made up her worldview.

Instead, Minsi saw the privilege of *Whiteness* from her perspective as a victim of inequalities rather than being a valued member of American society. She realized that being White and speaking English in and out of school validated people as *real Americans*. As a result, during Minsi's school years, she began to depart from her Chinese identity and native language. Inadvertently, these racial and cultural tensions have left Minsi disconnected from the purpose of schooling as it relates to her everyday realities as a Chinese American student from a low-income background.

EDUCATIONAL REALITIES OF URBAN CHINESE AMERICAN YOUTH

Within the past decade, 18 to 34 percent of New York City's Asian American students failed to complete high school in four years (New York City Department of Education, 2011). Contrary to the popular "model minority" stereotype that assumes all Asian American youth are successful students, a significant number of Asian Americans are not performing well in school (Teranishi, 2011).

Chinese Americans comprise the largest Asian American group in New York City. Yet, 33 percent of Chinese Americans do not have a high school degree, 22 percent have less than a ninth grade education, and 60 percent have limited English proficiency (Asian American Federation of New York, 2009). Studies have illustrated that poor/low-income Asian American youth from immigrant families and the first generation to attend the public school system are more likely to fail and drop out of school (Suárez-Orozco, Louie, & Suro, 2011).

Many poor/low-income Chinese American youth from immigrant communities—similar to Minsi—attend schools in which their lived experiences, culture, language, and Chinese American history are omitted or distorted in the standard history and social studies curriculum (Tintiangco-Cubales, Kiang, & Museus, 2010). As a result, these same Chinese American youth often feel isolated and disengaged from school because their classrooms lack a culturally relevant learning environment that affirms their everyday realities and connects them to their historical ties as ethnic Americans.

However, within underresourced minority communities there often exist community-based organizations that harness valuable youth organizations, which are responsive to the needs of minority youth. It has been argued that community-based after-school programs that center around minority youth's lived experiences, culture, and relevancy to American history are a strong component that can increase minority youth's engagement in school and civic participation in their community (Tintiangco-Cubales, Daus-Magbual, & Daus-Magbual, 2010). Minority youth demonstrate engagement and civic participation when their voices, perspectives, and historical or cultural back-grounds are validated.

CREATING SPACE FOR CHINESE AMERICAN YOUTH

Although Minsi's public school education was disconnected from her every-day life experiences, Minsi was able to find a community-based youth pro-gram in Chinatown known as Chinese American Youth Now! (CAYN!). CAYN! was a special place for Minsi and other low-income Chinese American youth who were not only seeking a place for academic support, but who also needed a space that allowed Chinese American youth to explore the challenges of social issues such as racism, immigration, poverty, and bicultu-ral tensions.

CAYN! became a haven for Minsi because this unique community-based youth program was socially and politically responsive to the significant num-ber of Chinese American youth who were disengaging, failing, and dropping out of school.

Minsi gravitated towards CAYN! not only because of the caring staff, but also because CAYN! developed a culturally relevant Chinese American his-tory after-school program that validated her real-life experiences and ethnic American history as scholarship. The educators at CAYN! valued the Chi-nese American youth's cultural characteristics such as their language, fami-ly's immigration, and ethnicity. They viewed these factors as significant assets in an effort to engage and empower Chinese American youth to criti-cally understand their life experiences, community, and history as Chinese Americans.

During the school year, Minsi participated in the Chinese American histo-ry after-school program at CAYN! once a week for two hours. She immersed herself in a room filled with 25 other high school students who were inter-ested in learning about their own daily realities, challenges, and history as Chinese Americans. In return for their participation, CAYN! provided the youth with numerous educational and networking resources. CAYN! af-forded participants high school tutoring, college guidance, workshops on career building, and an opportunity for a summer job at a New York City local agency.

These educational and career incentives helped Minsi and many others to participate in a Chinese American history after-school program that they may have otherwise declined due to their family's financial restraints. Many poor and struggling Chinese immigrant parents demand their children work after school in order to supplement their family's income. Recognizing that low-income Chinese American youth have financial concerns, CAYN! structured its after-school program to allow young people an opportunity to participate in an ethnic American history program that is fully committed to investing in their educational and economic future.

LEARNING ABOUT UNTOLD HISTORY

Janice Wong is Minsi's youth educator at CAYN!. Janice is a passionate scholar-activist who shared the same life and educational experiences as Minsi when she was younger. Due to Janice's close connection to all of her students' lived experiences, she has dedicated her teaching career to advance the educational experiences of low-income urban Chinese American youth. Janice developed a six-month Chinese American history program as a means to empower Chinese American youth to make sense of their sociocultural realities and to overcome their economic barriers.

The Chinese American history after-school curriculum and teaching practices are guided by a culturally relevant framework and critical multicultural perspective (May & Sleeter, 2010). Specifically, Janice uses three areas of a culturally relevant framework to link Chinese American youth's learning experiences shared among school, home, peers, and community.

First, Janice tells all participants that their life experiences and Chinese American history comprise a body of scholarship. Second, she informs her students that their Chinese heritage, culture, ethnicity, and languages are all valuable assets that contribute to their learning experiences and shape how they view the world. Finally, Janice advises the class that this after-school program is like no other class that they have ever taken in school.

She explains to the students that they are expected to analyze their in- and out-of-school experiences, community, and history by becoming social agents as a means to improve their own lives and the larger society. As an educator—and someone who walked in the same path as her own students— Janice knew that when Chinese American youth view the benefits of education for themselves and their community, they are more likely to care and become engaged both in and out of school.

The Chinese American history after-school program became a second home for Minsi and her peers because the program focused on building strong relationships among students; this enabled everyone in the group to be unified, which helped the youth construct and exchange their learning experiences together. Over time, Janice collaborated with the participants to develop a communal group structure that fostered friendship, trust, and respect among students and the instructor.

Minsi found the Chinese American history after-school program to be refreshing because Janice was able to open a new learning experience that was reflective and critical to the everyday realities of Chinese American youth in Chinatown. The after-school curriculum included a wide range of historical artifacts and materials that mirrored the interest of Chinese American youth today. For instance, Minsi had an opportunity to read traditional historical texts about Chinese Americans in the form of a journal article, excerpts from textbooks, and documentaries.

However, Janice also recognized the importance of incorporating historical materials and teaching practices that included the expressions of youth culture and minority perspectives of American history that may not be valued as official scholarship in school and society (Apple, 1979). For example, Minsi had the opportunity to listen to Chinese American history through the medium of hip-hop music—entitled "The Rest is History"—from Jin (2004), a Chinese American rapper.

During this exercise, Minsi listened to the rap song, jotted down words, and drew images that came to her mind. Classmates discussed and shared their responses with one another in small groups and then reported their findings to the class. For Minsi, listening to music and using it as a medium to understand and interpret American history was engaging. Minsi never learned about Chinese American history in school in this style before, nor has she ever had an opportunity to hear rap music written and performed by an Asian American artist.

At school, Minsi rarely has opportunities to voice her insights of American history. However, at the Chinese American history after-school program, the curriculum challenges youth to analyze historical events through their worldviews. Minsi and her peers frequently work together exploring issues such as race, class, and their own immigration experiences. Students engage in personal interviews, group presentations, bilingual theatrical skits, and open class discussions as a way to explore their daily realities.

These innovative examples of a critical multicultural curriculum and pedagogy in this after-school program illustrate a culturally relevant framework that conceptualizes low-income Chinese American youth and their Chinatown community as sources and producers of knowledge (Halagao, 2010; May & Sleeter, 2010). Valuing Chinese American youth's life experiences and family histories can encourage students from marginalized communities to become invested in themselves and their academic materials (Halagao).

LOOKING AT THE WORLD DIFFERENTLY

As the Chinese American history after-school program was coming to a close, Minsi appeared both somber and excited at the same time. After completing the program, she reflected on her learning and her Chinatown community with a renewed perspective. For the first time, Minsi became interested and engaged in learning at school. She had an affinity towards American history when it was told from the perspectives of Chinese

Americans, youth, and other minority groups. For once, Minsi's spark for learning was ignited when she saw herself and her Chinese ancestry represented in various historical media.

Minsi now scours bookstores around New York City and various Internet websites to research the history of Chinese Americans and community-based organizations that support young Asian Americans. She communicates with Janice over e-mail and Facebook, often citing her new findings of youth articles, books, music, poems, and movies that relate to Chinese American youth and Asian American history.

A LIFE TRANSFORMED

The Chinese American history after-school program gave Minsi an opportunity to examine American history as a body of scholarship that challenged the historical and sociopolitical experiences of people of color in the United States that have been traditionally concentrated in a Eurocentric perspective. She realized after participating in the Chinese American history after-school program that the experience became a transformative period in her school years. Minsi became aware that not only her critical consciousness had been impacted, but also her engagement and aspiration in school.

First, Minsi noticed that learning about Chinese American history alerted her to view the world from multiple perspectives, such as from those of the poor, women, and other people of color. Second, Minsi realized that exploring Chinese American history challenged her to critically examine school knowledge across race, class, gender, and cultures. She noted that many voices and experiences were omitted from her school learning and further questioned such educational injustices.

The after-school program influenced Minsi to make critical comparisons between the formal knowledge she was exposed to in school and the hidden curriculum. Minsi would often tell Janice,

> In our after-school program the activities and books we read would not be considered "classics" in school. It's not *Huckleberry Finn*, but what we read in our Chinese American history program is just as important as reading *Huckleberry Finn*. We read about our lives as Chinese American kids in Chinatown, children of immigrant parents, and even got a chance to perform in public about our everyday realities to people. America is made up of different people with diverse cultures, languages, and experiences; in our school everyone should get a chance to learn about it.

RECONSTRUCTING HISTORY FOR ALL YOUTH

Minsi's voice represents urban Asian American youth in search of a learning experience that is culturally relevant, meaningful, and socially responsive. Her story commands the attention of teachers, school officials, and community-based organizations to listen, to understand, and to respond to the complex lived experiences and engagement of low-income Chinese American youth.

Based on Minsi's experience in the Chinese American after-school program, it is urgent that school administrators, educators, and community-based organizations collaborate to develop culturally relevant teaching practices and critical multicultural curriculum that is reflective of the ethnic American history and lives of all students. Furthermore, based on the increasing number of Asian American youth disengaging, failing, and dropping out of school from underresourced communities, there is a dire need for culturally relevant and critical multicultural curriculum to be implemented in public schools and community-based after-school programs in order to facilitate youth's engagement in and out of school.

Minsi's experiences at CAYN! may inform educators and community-based leaders that there are significant academic and social outcomes for minority students when there is a strong relationship between schools and community-based organizations. Such resourceful partnerships can improve the public schools' standard curriculum and teaching practices that are critical and reflective of the daily realities and ethnic American history of minority students. In doing so, the overarching goal to support *all* youth in developing a diverse perspective of American history and a global society will be met.

NOTE

All names are pseudonyms.

REFERENCES

Apple, M. W. (1979). *Ideology and curriculum.* London, UK: Routledge & Kegan Paul.
Asian American Federation of New York. (2009). *Census profile: New York City's Chinese American population.* New York, NY: Asian American Federation of New York Census Information Center.
Halagao, P. E. (2010). Liberating Filipino Americans through decolonizing curriculum. *Race Ethnicity and Education 13*, 495–512.
Jin. (Writer) (2004). *The rest is history.* USA: Virgin Records US.
May, S., & Sleeter, C. E. (2010). *Critical multiculturalism: Theory and praxis.* New York, NY: Routledge.
New York City Department of Education. (2011). *New York City graduation rates: Class of 2010.* New York, NY: Author.

Suárez-Orozco, M. M., Louie, V., & Suro, R. (2011). *Writing immigration: Scholars and journalists in dialogue.* Berkeley, CA: University of California Press.

Teranishi, R. (2011). *The relevance of Asian Americans & Pacific Islanders in the college completion agenda.* New York, NY: National Commission on Asian American and Pacific Islander Research in Education.

Tintiangco-Cubales, A., Daus-Magbual, R., & Daus-Magbual, A. (2010). Pin@y educational partnership: A counter-pipeline to create critical educators. *Asian American Pacific Islander Nexus, 8*(1), 76–100.

Tintiangco-Cubales, A., Kiang, P. N., & Museus, S. D. (2010). Praxis and power in the intersections of education. *Asian American Pacific Islander Nexus, 8*(1), v–xvii.

Chapter Seventeen

Raising Engagement and Enhancing Learning: School Community Partnerships that Work for Students "At-Promise"

David Zyngier

OUR LOCAL CONTEXT

We live in a society where—despite widespread concerns about children and teenagers—the vast majority of adults are not actively involved in the lives of young people outside of their own families. This reality has a profound impact on community life and on young people's development. Without the attention of many adults in all parts of their lives and community, young people are deprived of important sources of guidance, nurture, care, and socialization. (Scales, Benson, & Mannes, 2002, p. ix)

When the education faculty at my university received an e-mail asking if anyone was interested in setting up a "homework club or the like" at a local elementary school there were very few takers. But Noble Elementary was no ordinary school—on the outskirts of eastern Melbourne with most families coming from low socioeconomic backgrounds, with 40 nationalities and 36 languages spoken in the school—Noble Elementary was a microcosm of multicultural Australia. Three quarters of its pupils are from non-English speaking backgrounds with many recent refugees from Africa and Asia making up a significant proportion of the school population.

After contacting Principal David by phone it was clear this was not about a homework program at all! He told us that

> the idea is for those students who are perhaps not doing as well as they could, it could be bright kids who are in the program as well... It's not for under performance or the kids who are low achievers, it's for kids who perhaps could have the bar raised for them. I call it vicarious learning, because school for a lot of these kids is a bit of a pain. We don't want to replicate school again, so they're doing more school stuff.

Having been recognized by the Education Department of Victoria as an outstanding principal, David was granted time to work with Dr. George Otero from the Centre for Relational Learning in New Mexico. There he was introduced to the exciting and innovative work being conducted through Citizens School (2009).

Working with Monash University as a partner, we developed a community engagement program, the Enhanced Learning Improvement in Networked Communities (E-LINCs), which is an innovative project that partners university and community volunteers with schools where student learning difficulties and disengagement are significant issues.

Using theories of community strengths, we supported teachers "meeting and partnering with community members and agencies, to learn about the important community strengths that can be utilized in a more culturally relevant education" (Noel, 2010, p. 10). We wanted to know whether a program like this could have an impact on student engagement levels and the learning and social outcomes of students we call "at-promise" (Swadener, 1995), a far more positive term rather than the negative and deficit labeling of children "at-risk."

OUR CHALLENGE

The principal wanted to supplement the lack of social, economic, and cultural capital at the school and with its families through the use of university volunteers by challenging "the school context in which the young people are located" (Stewart, 1998, p. 4). We called this transformative approach *pedagogical reciprocity* in which the teachers and students could learn together and from each other (Zyngier, 2011). The program was not designed for any particular student type, as Principal David explained that "our aim is to have as many children who want to be involved, as well as those who need to be involved because there's no reason why children who aren't already doing well, can't even do better."

THEORETICAL FRAMEWORK: PARTNERSHIPS THAT ENHANCE SOCIAL CAPITAL

The problem of culturally, linguistically, and economically disenfranchised (CLED) children's disengagement from academic learning is well documented (Ladson-Billings, 2007; Villegas & Lucas, 2007) and was evident in the primary schools involved in the project. The teachers and administration worked hard and were extremely dedicated to their children in the school.

Like many schools in the state education system in Victoria, Noble Elementary suffered from lack of funds, dilapidated buildings, and limited access to resources that could make a difference to the children. We understood from the work of the Citizens School that education must not be considered the work of schools in isolation from their communities. Principal David was excited by the opportunity to create a cultural shift away from previously isolated and entrenched modes of working towards a more inclusive and holistic partnerships in education.

Yosso (2005) developed the concept of *community cultural wealth* which "focuses on and learns from the array of cultural knowledge, skills and abilities, and contacts possessed by socially marginalized groups that often go unrecognized, and unacknowledged" (p. 69). Noble Elementary increasingly was looking to communities and their funds of knowledge (Moll, Amanti, Neff, & Gonzalez, 1992) to help build capacity and improve educational outcomes.

Principal David emphasized the importance of young people having access to social capital and a network of social supports that would connect them to shared values, information, guidance, and contacts—all of which are critical for children who may have not been exposed to them in their homes due to circumstances of poverty, language, or immigration. "Each individual needs to belong to a 'community of practice' where beliefs are shared, skills are learned, and collective resources and interactions hold them together" (Melaville, Berg, & Blank, 2006, p. 20).

Our discussions reinforced our understanding that a strong school–community partnership could lead to better school attendance, quality school programs, improved student behavior, and discipline. The principal understood that effective school–community partnerships could give Noble Elementary a much broader range of resources and support networks on which to draw to benefit his students. In order to ensure this connection, he insisted that

> one of the fundamentals of the program is that at the end of the program there's a public celebration, it's very, very important, so that the children can show their parents and other siblings and their peers, as well as their other teachers, what we have achieved. So there's a public acknowledgement of it.

He convinced us that a partnership between his school and our university could play an important role in addressing some of the nonacademic barriers to learning, such as poor peer relations, family conflict and instability, negative community norms, and disorganization (Anderson-Butcher, Stetler, & Midle, 2006).

OUR INTERVENTION PROGRAM: ENHANCED LEARNING

When we visited Noble Elementary it was clear that the students' literacy development was often lower than expected for the age level, which means that functioning successfully in the classroom and obtaining skills and knowledge were difficult for them, their teachers, and peers. Our major goal was to establish an effective, on-going and well-attended after-school program for any students who were underachieving and/or disengaged, and who volunteered to attend in order to improve their learning.

The programs ran for eight weeks with sessions from 3:30 pm to 5:30 pm twice weekly. The afternoon started with volunteers playing some vigorous outside games with the children to *shake out the sillies* before sitting down together with adults for a communal afternoon tea to recharge their batteries.

Children then had the option to either complete set homework or work towards their chosen learning goals. The majority, in choosing the latter, were excused from homework completion, opting for learning goals as diverse as story writing, project work, spelling, handwriting, or numeracy activities, such as multiplication or computer skills. The volunteers assisted with these choices, which the children's parents would not have been able to help with at their homes.

After one hour of games, food, and individual work on learning goals or homework, the groups participated in enhanced learning that included student choice opportunities in educationally rich activities. The volunteers developed the following twice-weekly Enhanced Learning Workshops that included activities as diverse as claymation; music, dance and drama; everyday science; everyday cooking; digital photography and moviemaking; and art and mural development.

EVIDENCE OF SUCCESS

We documented, through photography, video and audio recording, the diverse projects developed by volunteers at Noble Elementary. We also conducted focus groups with school pupils, as well as surveyed and interviewed volunteers.

Most of the volunteers were from White, middle class backgrounds and commented positively (and with some surprise) about working with CLED children for the first time and stated that getting to know and understand students from different backgrounds and being involved with a school where there is so much diversity was a great experience.

The volunteers understood that student disengagement was a real issue for them to tackle and commented about their experiences with the children as they observed the changes in children's engagement levels during the program. The students loved the program because it built strong relationships that empowered them to tell us if they thought the program needed changing or how to improve it. It was clear that the students were really engaged and loved the activities and even loved doing their homework because of the help they received.

Seeing the students grow to trust us and enjoy the program, in particular seeing them apply themselves, was really rewarding. The children, too, were thrilled to give their feedback about the activities they did saying that,

- It's really fun. We had a photo hunt. And we made post cards. We made our own videos. It's funny, it's fun, yeah.
- I'm happy because I get lots of fun work. I don't like boring work.
- I learnt my division.
- Now I know how to make harder experiments and they're actually easy.
- It helped me for class and for life as well. It was really fun and it makes me get more active instead of sitting at home and watching TV... or turning on the computer.

According to Principal David, many children were also now attending school regularly for the first time because they did not want to miss the twice weekly sessions with the university students. One particular child was the *sick bay girl* who teachers described as living in the sick bay and who would not participate in class whatsoever. After a few sessions of Enhanced Learning, she was becoming more involved in the class activities and always had a smile on her face. The child's teacher said that she taught her whole class one of the sessions she had learned during Enhanced Learning and has become more involved in class.

The volunteers also reflected on the program and its positive effect on the students. Seeing children work hard on their learning goals because they really want to understand the work was very impressive. One child was confident that she could now even "Tell my teacher how to make tornadoes in bottles and, slime, and how to make the lava lamp."

The volunteers spoke passionately about the positive change they saw in just eight weeks in these grade 5 and 6 children. As Gemma wrote "the students are glad to have us there to help them with their homework and ask lots of questions and I believe they have become more confident in completing their work."

Other volunteers alluded to the lack of necessary cultural and social capital at home that the program now provided:

> Seeing themselves improve in their performance skills and actually being given time and help with doing their homework which they told us they do not get at home was important. We had no trouble getting them to do their work as we provided a place for them to have fun and be themselves, they weren't in any competition with each other, as they were all different.

Through the program many of the children had changed from shy underachievers, often seemingly ashamed of their cultural backgrounds, to having much higher aspirations for themselves. The students began to believe that now anything might be possible. One child told us that Enhanced Learning "helps me to learn, they help us with our homework. It's really exciting because I'm really excited, like if I grow up I'll be a scientist or something."

Principal David, noting previous school data, was clear that these children were hard to keep engaged in their traditional school environment, but their teachers, the principal, and volunteers agreed that the children had all been fully engaged in this program. He was able to identify individuals who made enormous strides, pointing out one child at the school presentation who

> was a very, very shy kid, but during that program, you could see his engagement level was really, really high, and he was actually experiencing success, where he's normally one of those kids who would be sitting in the background and making himself as inconspicuous as possible.

Our purpose was to use Enhanced Learning as a part of a strategy to build social capital, enhance learning, and develop powerful learning relationships. We knew we were succeeding when we heard one child tell us that "We can show our parents how to do what we do at school and how we do it and the purpose is that we can take it home and do it."

Coming from the belief that it takes a village to raise a child, the project provided a space where young people can learn new skills and grow their own self-worth, and community members can share expertise, building on the collective community knowledge of the young people by improving their experiential base. The project engaged disadvantaged "at-promise" youth in authentic learning.

Kelvin identified the impact in this way when he wrote that when the university volunteers

> saw the children's faces light up and call their names from across the asphalt when they arrived at school they understood that the impact that the community partnership had and the children could not wait to share about something that was important to them. We were able to see their personalities come out

when we listened to them talk at the end of each session about what they achieved and what they liked about the session.

DISCUSSION

By adding to the community's social and cultural capital, this program has the potential for the children to change their own lives, thereby fulfilling their *promise*. This program has been successful because of its multilevel approach that required buy-in from teachers, researchers, the community, and other young people to make it a success. This innovative program to re-engage underachieving students was at a minimal cost to the community and clearly proved to be a positive alternative model to other expensive and unsuccessful intervention programs.

At the core of this successful program was the need for all participants to feel they were empowered. We now know that student outcomes can be enhanced when the students feel connected to and involved in their community (Epstein, Galindo, & Sheldon, 2011).

Through this project, the students had the opportunity to experience greater community engagement leading to improved school attendance and retention, as well as better academic outcomes. As a result, the program was awarded two competitive national awards for its significant contribution to Australian education.

CONCLUSION

Principal David explained that

> we can't set kids on that path of thinking about what they do in a normal primary school, but you can start to develop interests that are not necessarily going to be developed in the run of the mill school day, and particularly with the backgrounds they come from in our area, they're not necessarily that aspirational.

We have now developed an ongoing productive partnership between Noble Elementary and our university (Otero, Csoti, & Rothstadt, 2011). This has affected inclusive teaching and learning practices at the school and at the university level. But more significantly, it has demonstrated that such an intervention has the potential to have an impact on engagement levels as well as the learning and social outcomes of students from refugee, migrant, and working class families, enabling them to achieve their potential, their promise. All the participants were empowered to enhance outcomes because students felt connected to and involved in their community (Zyngier, 2003).

NOTE

All names are pseudonyms.

REFERENCES

Anderson-Butcher, D., Stetler, E. G., & Midle, T. (2006). A case for expanded school–community partnerships in support of positive youth development. *Children & Schools, 28*, 155–163.

Citizen Schools. (2009). *Our model.* Retrieved from http://www.citizenschools.org/whatwedo/ourmodel/

Epstein, J. L., Galindo, C. L., & Sheldon, S. B. (2011). Levels of leadership effects of district and school leaders on the quality of school programs of family and community involvement. *Educational Administration Quarterly, 47*, 462–495.

Ladson-Billings, G. (2007). Culturally responsive teaching: Theory and practice. *Multicultural education: Issues and perspectives, 6*, 219–246.

Melaville, A., Berg, A. C., & Blank, M. J. (2006). *Community-based learning: Engaging students for success and citizenship.* Washington, DC: Coalition for Community Schools.

Moll, L. C., Amanti, C., Neff, D., & Gonzalez, N. (1992). Funds of knowledge for teaching: Using a qualitative approach to connect homes and classrooms. *Theory Into Practice, 31*, 132–141.

Noel, J. (2010). Weaving teacher education into the fabric of urban schools. *Teacher Education Quarterly, 37*(3), 9–25.

Otero, G., Csoti, R., & Rothstadt, D. (2011). *Creating powerful learning relationships: A whole school community approach.* Cheltenham, Australia: Hawker Brownlow Education.

Scales, P., Benson, P., & Mannes, M. (2002). *Grading grown-ups 2002: How do American kids and adults relate? Key findings from a national study.* Minneapolis, MN: Lutheran Brotherhood and Search Institute.

Stewart, H. (October 1998). At risk or marginalised? The implications of focussing on at risk individual young people for workers with marginalised young people. *YACVic Bits, 1,* 4–5.

Swadener, B. B. (1995). Children and families "at promise": Deconstructing the discourse of risk. In B. B. Swadener & S. Lubeck (Eds.), *Children and families "at promise": Deconstructing the discourse of risk* (pp. 17–49). Albany, NY: State University of New York Press.

Villegas, A. M., & Lucas, T. (2007). The culturally responsive teacher. *Educational Leadership, 64*(6), 6.

Yosso, T. (2005). Whose culture has capital? A critical race theory discussion of community cultural wealth. *Race, Ethnicity and Education, 8*(1), 69–91.

Zyngier, D. (2003). Connectedness: Isn't it time that education came out from behind the classroom door and rediscovered social justice. *Social Alternatives, 22*(3), 41–49.

Zyngier, D. (2011). (Re)conceptualising risk: Left numb and unengaged and lost in a no-man's-land or what (seems to) work for at-risk students. *International Journal of Inclusive Education, 15*, 211–231.

Chapter Eighteen

Montessori High Schools: Where Long-Standing Tradition Meets the Cutting Edge

Wendy J. LaRue and Peter Hoffman-Kipp

LEAVING OUR CHILDREN BEHIND

Would-be school reformers have spent the last decade encouraging competition, comparison, and so-called tougher standards in the name of leaving no child in the United States behind. The standards-based education system that No Child Left Behind (2002) and other related reform efforts perpetuate has failed to meet the needs of 21st century students. Extensive and expensive testing programs and initiatives such as school choice have not improved school quality. Students are continuing to graduate from high school ill-prepared for higher education and the 21st century workplace.

These points were driven home when education historian Diane Ravitch (2010), who for the past decade was a staunch advocate for high-stakes testing and school choice, declared she no longer believed either approach would bring about substantial improvement of public education. Ravitch argued the rigid curriculum and boring textbooks that have supported this failed approach must be traded for an education system that promotes active learning, critical thinking, creativity, innovation, and imagination.

LOOKING FOR A NEW PATH

Having failed to achieve the desired results, the current framework of U.S. high schools needs to be put aside. It is time to examine novel approaches to school improvement, and U.S. Montessori high schools offer a model for student-centered reform that is worthy of consideration. The Montessori high school movement, although still in its infancy, is rooted in the more than 100-year-long legacy of Montessori education and provides an example of an ideal combination of (a) self-paced, student-centered learning; (b) congenial and even family-like relationships between students and adults; (c) hands-on, experiential learning opportunities; and (d) authentic connections to the adult world.

The number of Montessori high schools in the United States is small; however, these institutions offer a promising glimpse at what secondary education could be. Examining five programs (one public, two charter, two private) of the approximately 30 U.S. Montessori high schools offered insight into how these innovative programs are creating groundbreaking communities in which independent learning skills flourish, skills for the 21st century are nurtured, and students' social and emotional development receive the attention they merit (LaRue, 2011).

While their traditional school counterparts are preparing for a relentless barrage of standardized tests, Montessori high school students are creating their own elective classes, tailoring their learning objectives to their personal interests, using their entire communities as their classrooms, creating microbusinesses, planning extended field studies, and developing workplace skills through internships. These programs build on the longstanding foundation of Montessori tradition, while they simultaneously provide educational opportunities that are on the cutting edge.

MONTESSORI SECONDARY SCHOOLS IN THEORY

Montessori secondary programs are intended to be a continuation of the early childhood and elementary levels. As such, the secondary programs focus on meeting the unique needs of adolescents and provide students not only a quality academic program, but also a hands-on exploration of the adult world in which they are preparing to live. By providing true whole-child learning opportunities, these programs aim "to put the adolescent on the road to achieving economic independence" (p. 64), which was Montessori's (1948/1994) stated goal of secondary education.

Montessori (1948/1994) suggested that authentic work is key in helping prepare students to meet the goal of becoming financially independent. The emphasis on work is simply a continuation of the mission of the earlier levels of Montessori education and is analogous to the Montessori practical life lessons such as spooning, pouring, and dressing that allow early childhood students to gain the independence they crave with regard to meeting their physical needs.

Montessori posited the ideal context for doing real work was a farm school setting, where adolescents could derive the physical health benefits of life in the outdoors and of fresh nutritious food, while enjoying the mental health benefits of peace and wonder that the tranquil environment inspires (Montessori, 1948/1994). This notion is known as the Erdkinder Model among Montessorians, named for the title of an essay Montessori wrote in an appendix to *From Childhood to Adolescence.* Montessori argued schools should provide adolescents indoctrination into society by offering opportunities to make authentic contributions to the community, and she believed place-based education was the conduit for doing so.

Though a farm school complete with a market and a hostel as Montessori described (1948/1994) may not be practical in most 21st century communities, principles of place-based pedagogy can be applied in any setting. Kemp (2006) noted place-based learning provides a starting point for studying universal concepts by first examining them in the local community: "A curriculum that starts with a place and expands to the world would enable students to understand each better" (p. 140).

The work of Helen Parkhurst, Montessori's most trusted protégé, provides a basis for many Montessori high school programs as well (Lee, 2000; Seldin & Epstein, 2003). Parkhurst developed her Dalton Laboratory Plan to foster independent learning and peer teaching while providing opportunities for meaningful involvement in the school community and the community at-large. Under the Dalton Plan, students manage their own time and learning in order to complete open-ended assignments, which develops self-motivated, self-directed learners (Lee, 2000). Respect for students lies at the heart of the Dalton Plan, just as it does for Montessori education, with freedom, cooperation, and self-imposed budgeting of time being the core components (Lee).

Montessori (1948/1994) noted that adaptability is essential in a world where change occurs continually and where new careers are arising while others are being revolutionized or eliminated; thus, Montessori secondary programs aim to foster adaptability in the students. Self-expression through music, language, and art should be presented in a combination of both individual opportunities and cooperative group activities, according to Montessori, and the nature of the work should involve free choice. Montessori's education plan for secondary students included moral education, mathematics, language, the study of the earth and all living things, the study of human progress and civilization, and the study of history of mankind.

Montessori (1948/1994) advocated a setting in which students have the opportunity for meaningful experiences that include clear-cut goals and genuine feedback. Csikszentmihalyi (1990) described these characteristics as *flow experiences*. These optimal experiences allow individuals to commit themselves fully to achieving goals "because there is no disorder to straighten out, no threat for the self to defend" (Csikszentmihalyi, p. 40). While

Montessori advocated a farm setting for fostering these experiences, Seldin and Epstein (2003) noted that the setting does not necessarily have to be a farm school, which would be altogether impractical as a large-scale model for public school reform.

The most important feature of a Montessori high school is neither the location of the school nor the curriculum, but rather the manner in which students are treated. From the perspective of one who saw the adolescent soul as a vessel of hope for the future of humanity, Montessori asserted that adolescents should never be treated as if they are children, because they have moved beyond that stage of life (Montessori, 1948/1994). She stated, "It is better to treat an adolescent as if he had greater value than he actually shows than as if he had less and let him feel that his merits and self-respect are disregarded" (Montessori, p. 73).

Theory that underlies current practice in Montessori high schools, which is consistent with themes in the literature regarding 21st century skills, provides a framework that possesses enormous promise for helping to shape widespread high school reform. Before educators can consider how Montessori high school pedagogical practices might be implemented to improve high school instruction, they must understand the practices themselves, and the context in which they are implemented. This case study provides the first vital step in creating a conceptual framework of Montessori high school education.

MONTESSORI HIGH SCHOOL IN PRACTICE

The data from our case study of five Montessori high schools, which included urban, suburban, and rural settings, suggest several components of Montessori practice that have potential for use in creating the kind of reforms Ravitch (2010) suggested. These program components address the need for active learning, critical thinking, creativity, innovation, and imagination. Montessori secondary schools' hands-on approach to instruction provides opportunities for higher level thinking.

The give-and-take environment in which teachers and students are learning together is exemplified in Montessori high schools, and appears to support strong relationships between students and teachers. The interest in individual students' learning may be a factor that minimizes the negative effects of assessment techniques such as grades and standardized tests (Golden, Kist, Trehan, & Padak, 2005) and creates the collegial (rather than competitive or didactic) relationships that appear to characterize the Montessori high school experience.

The Erdkinder Model

None of the programs follow the Erdkinder model (Montessori, 1948/1994) precisely; yet all five schools incorporate elements of the plan. Three of the five specifically include a farm program. One of the schools that does not include a farm program has a boarding component. The fifth school offers a course specifically intended to create Erdkinder-like business experiences in the urban, public school setting. All of the programs incorporate opportunities for students to gain skills for economic independence through service learning and internships.

We found compelling evidence that adolescents develop the concept of empathy and begin to experience society independently, as well as develop self-respect through place-based work. In other words, the opportunities for authentic work and authentic contribution to the local and global community assist Montessori high school students in meeting the developmental needs of adolescence as they work to gain skills to become members of adult society.

Not only Montessori (1948/1994), but also Dewey (1902/1990), maintained that during adolescence the learning environment must surpass the confines of the classroom. Smith (2002) posited that meaningful education is directly related to the students' own social reality. The opportunities Montessori high schools provide for place-based learning, through internships and service work, support a broad social perspective with diverse benefits. Both student and staff participants in our study frequently emphasized that at their schools experiential opportunities focus not only on intellectual development, but also social, emotional, and spiritual development.

Our findings suggest that (a) the integrated curriculum, which encourages students to make connections in their learning, (b) the freedom students are afforded in the classroom, (c) the caring relationships that are forged between students and teachers, and (d) the experiential approach to learning work in tandem to relate the education experiences to the students' roles in society, thus meeting their developmental needs.

Means for incorporating Erdkinder concepts into Montessori high schools will undoubtedly continue to evolve. Montessori (1918/1991) developed early childhood and elementary programs through mindful observation of children at work, and contemporary Montessorians will need to do the same by observing students in their varied learning venues. "It was thus that the soul of the child gave its revelations, and under their guidance a method exemplifying spiritual liberty was evolved" (Montessori, 1918/1991, p. 54), and it is thus that the adolescent's soul will similarly guide Erdkinder methodology.

Preparing Students for Higher Education and Adult Work

Montessori high schools, as demonstrated by the five schools discussed here, gear curriculum specifically to prepare students for higher education and adult work. Integrated curriculum fosters higher level thinking needed for success in both postsecondary venues. The class structure of the Montessori high schools provides autonomy for students, yet encourages interdependence as well. Egalitarian relationships among students and staff as well as the expectation that students hold responsibility for their learning also foster skills for higher education and adult work.

Comparing High Schools to Other Levels of Montessori Education

All of the characteristics of traditional Montessori education that we considered (multiage classroom, prepared environment, authentic assessment, self-directed learning, experiential learning, emphasis on the natural world, and close relationships between students and teachers) had some role in the Montessori high schools. Regardless of the structure in the classroom, community interaction through internships and service work greatly expands the age range of those with whom students regularly interact and support Montessori's belief that adolescents should be afforded opportunities to integrate themselves into the adult community.

Many of the responsibilities for preparing the environment are relinquished to the students at the high school level, where adolescents are likely to not only assist with configuring and maintaining the classroom and school, but also seeking personally meaningful environments in the greater community for their studies. While comparison and traditional grading are not norms for early childhood and elementary programs, all five Montessori high schools use grades. In most cases, the approach to grading was more flexible than in traditional environments, and in all cases grading was implemented in an effort to facilitate university matriculation.

Self-directed learning, experiential learning, and focus on the natural world were a part of all five of the programs. At the three schools that offered farm-based programs, there was a particular emphasis on experiential learning in nature. Older students at those schools, as well as students at schools with no farm component, still had learning experiences that incorporated these characteristics extensively. Ives and Obenchain (2006) identified this type of education as supporting use of higher order thinking skills.

One of the most notable characteristics of Montessori high schools is the relationships between students and staff and among students. A give-and-take environment in which teachers and students are learning together, and in which relationships are characterized by a sense of family, was prominently evident in all five cases.

Some examples of this quality are as follows:

- We call every teacher by their first name and some of the students even joke around with certain teachers like they were classmates. This is drastically different from my grade school, but I love it.
- If we have trouble we can go right up and talk about it with our teachers, and that's what I like about our school.
- We're like brothers and sisters. We're like family here. Then I look at my cousin who goes to a public school in [a nearby town]. She talks about all these people, but she's just friends. Do you know what I mean?
- I do think they have strong healthy adult–student relationships where they can trust the staff. They can go to the staff with difficult issues. They can go to the staff with concerns. So I'm really pleased with the adult–student relationship.
- We use first names. That freaks a lot of people out. They call us by our first names. They come to our houses.
- Students are very comfortable with being not only socially close, but also physically close. I often notice that kids are holding hands like Europeans. It's just very comfortable and intimate.

SEEDS FOR SCHOOL REFORM

Common threads among the programs are not related to specific didactic materials or core content. This might be the case for Montessori early childhood or elementary programs for which there is a century of history, an extensive written legacy, a vast array of scientifically created and selected materials, and a network of training programs aimed at preparing Montessorians to practice their art in a precise and uncompromising manner.

Instead, the common threads are (a) focus on social, emotional, spiritual, and intellectual development; (b) integrated curriculum; (c) opportunities for experiential education, student-centered learning, and authentic adult work; and (d) family-like teacher/student relationships. The structure of the communities and the nature of the relationships within them appear to be the elements that give the schools a Montessori feel, even though there is a great deal of variation regarding curriculum, instruction, and assessment. This finding is especially encouraging in terms of the potential for creating broad school reform based on this research.

IMPLICATIONS FOR THE FUTURE

Emulating the models examined in the five participating schools would have a number of benefits to society. First, if students were provided greater opportunities for using more critical thinking, cooperation, and collaboration, they might be better prepared for higher education and an adult occupation in the 21st century, or be college and career ready (Common Core, 2012). If all areas of development were nurtured, students might feel more connected to their learning, to their community, and to humanity, because they would be supported in developing a deeper understanding of the web of life.

If students were provided plentiful opportunities to increase their self-worth through authentic work via service learning and internships, they would be better prepared to be good stewards of themselves, other people, and the environment. And finally, if schools provided a system in which deep personal relationships between students and teachers were supported rather than thwarted, students might be more vested in their education for the short term and the long haul. Implementing the practices observed as essential in the five schools discussed here could benefit educators and students alike by creating an environment where, through side-by-side learning, everyone's needs are more likely to be satisfied.

CALL TO ACTION

More than 60 years ago, Montessori (1948/1994) wrote,

> Schools as they are today, are adapted neither to the needs of adolescence nor to the times in which we live… the schools have remained in a kind of arrested development, organized in a way that cannot have been well suited even to the needs of the past, but that today is actually in contrast with human progress. (p. 59)

Ironically, this indictment of secondary education is even more relevant today, given that there has been no widespread change in school structure despite continued and rapid changes in the way we live. It is time to break the mold of high school education and turn to innovative approaches, such as Montessori education, for meeting the developmental needs of adolescents and preparing them for adult life in the 21st century.

REFERENCES

Common Core State Standards Initiative. (2012). Retrieved from http://www.corestandards.org
Csikszentmihalyi, M. (1990). *Flow: The psychology of optimal experience.* New York, NY: Harper.

Dewey, J. (1902/1990). *The school and society & the child and the curriculum.* Chicago, IL: The University of Chicago.

Golden, S., Kist, W., Trehan, D. M., & Padak, N. (2005). A teacher's words are tremendously powerful: Stories from the GED Scholars Initiative. *Phi Delta Kappan, 87*, 311–315.

Ives, B., & Obenchain, K. (2006). Experiential education in the classroom and academic outcomes: For those who want everything. *Journal of Experiential Education, 29*, 61–77.

Kemp, A. (2006). Engaging the environment. *Curriculum & Teaching Dialogue, 8*(1/2), 125–142.

LaRue, W. J. (2011). *Empowering adolescents: A multiple case study of U.S. Montessori high schools.* Retrieved from http://amshq.org/Publications%20and%20Research/Research%20Library/Dissertations%20and%20Theses.aspx

Lee, L. F. (2000). The Dalton Plan and the loyal, capable intelligent citizen. *History of Education, 29*, 129–138.

Montessori, M. (1918/1991). *The advanced Montessori method I.* Oxford, UK: Clio Press.

Montessori, M. (1948/1994). *From childhood to adolescence.* Oxford, UK: Clio Press.

No Child Left Behind Act of 2001, Pub. L. No. 107–110, Section 601 (2002).

Ravitch, D. (2010). *The death and life of the great American school system: How testing and choice are undermining education.* New York, NY: Basic Books.

Seldin, T., & Epstein, P. (2003). *The Montessori way.* Sarasota, FL: The Montessori Foundation Press.

Smith, G. (2002). Place-based education. *Phi Delta Kappan, 83*, 584–594.

Chapter Nineteen

Ma te Mahi e Ako Ai (Learning by Doing in New Zealand Higher Education): The Influence of Service-Learning on Student Engagement

Lane Perry, Billy O'Steen, and Peter Cammock

In 2007, at a full classroom in the engineering block at the University of Canterbury campus, the question and answer session of the road show on sustainability, organized by then Parliamentary Commissioner for the Environment, Dr. Morgan Williams, was underway. He had prepared a panel of eminent international experts on sustainability. Professors Trevor and David were among the audience members.

During the question and answer session, they were struck by two young women students in the middle of the room who asked, "Why is it that university is all about talking at us, and why can't we get out and be doing useful things? What is the point in talking about sustainability all the time, rather than actually doing it?" More so than the focus on sustainability, it was the "getting out and doing useful things... actually doing it" that sparked Trevor's and David's interest. It was this question that served as a catalyst for these academicians to rework an upper-level course with the purpose of heeding these two young women's call.

Trevor has described himself, and has been recognized, as a teacher who is one to never stand still when it comes to teaching and learning methods. He likes to keep experimenting with new ideas and strategies. Not because, "doing things different is better, but there are always new things that you can try in order to obtain new objectives."

David shares a similar perspective regarding teaching and learning. "Teaching is not really the important thing. It is the students' learning, so it is more like facilitating learning [than teaching]." In these perspectives, David and Trevor recognize that in a facilitative role, different methods of teaching can be adopted to influence the students' learning environment in a positive way. It was this instinctive awareness, along with the opportune scenario introduced above, that led to the development and implementation of service-learning pedagogy into their upper-level UNIV300: Research Methods course.

This chapter focuses on the experiences of students within this service-learning classroom and serves as the source for this narrative. The conclusion illuminates what it was about these experiences within service-learning that fostered student engagement, growth, an enhanced academic environment, and a new sense of community awareness.

POURING THE FOUNDATION: MIXING SERVICE-LEARNING PEDAGOGY WITH EXPERIENTIAL EDUCATION PHILOSOPHY

It is the foundation of a structure that supports its greater purpose. The foundation for this study, which has been mixed, poured, and investigated by both researchers and practitioners, is the departure point for better under-standing and contextualizing a particular tertiary-based global perspective on the use of service-learning pedagogy and its subsequent influence on student engagement.

The links between service-learning theory and Dewey's philosophy of experiential education are wide and deep (Giles & Eyler, 1994). While Dewey never wrote specifically about service-learning, he did address many of the characteristics that describe the contemporary practice of it when he stated that "typical problems to be solved by personal reflection, experimen-tation and by acquiring definite bodies of knowledge leading later to more specialized scientific knowledge" (Dewey, 1933, pp. 290–291).

Since community is a core concept in Dewey's social philosophy and experience is a core concept in his education philosophy (Giles & Eyler, 1994), it is clear that experience for and with the community, so long as it is educative, could be seen as a logical implementation of his philosophies (Perry, 2011).

Building upon these ideas, Giles and Eyler (1994) further suggested that, "principles of continuity and interaction, the process of problematization and inquiry, and the phases of reflective thought" (p. 80) encompass the general concept of service-learning. Furthermore, in a higher education context, Parker, Myers, Higgins, Oddsson, Price, and Gould (2009) found that ser-vice-learning is of "considerable value to students and that well-defined re-search on CSL [service-learning], and its theorizing within university peda-gogy, is warranted" (p. 586).

BUILDING A FRAME WITH THEORETICAL AND EMPIRICAL SCAFFOLDS: STUDENT ENGAGEMENT AND SERVICE-LEARNING

Student engagement theory focuses on the relationship between students' involvement and university conditions and is underpinned by the most robust indicators of good practice in undergraduate teaching and learning (Chickering & Gamson, 1987, as cited in Nelson Laird, Chen, & Kuh, 2008). For example, student engagement is defined as "students' involvement with activities and conditions likely to generate high-quality learning" (Australian Council for Educational Research, 2008, p. 1). Kuh, Kinzie, Buckley, Bridges, and Hayek (2007) described student engagement as having two critical features:

> The first is the *amount of time and effort students put into their studies and other educationally purposeful activities...* The second is *how the institution deploys its resources and organizes the curriculum, other learning opportunities, and support services to induce students to participate in activities* that lead to the experiences and desired outcomes such as persistence, satisfaction, learning, and graduation. (p. 44, italics added)

According to Kuh, Kinzie, Schuh, and Whitt (2005), seamless student engagement in teaching and learning processes has been identified as a key factor for student success in higher education. Also, certain practices have been empirically shown to foster high levels of engagement (Kuh, 2008). This is where pedagogy such as service-learning—as a method promoting seamless student engagement—fits into the student engagement equation.

Other factors in the student engagement equation are two surveys being used in the world today—the National and Australasian Surveys of Student Engagement (NSSE & AUSSE). These surveys use theoretically and empirically derived measures of engagement and have been used by nearly 1,500 higher-education institutions and administered to over 2.5 million students in the US, Canada, and Australasia (Kuh, 2009).

By their widespread adoption and promotion of scores, these participating institutions are interested in student engagement and are, presumably, seeking ways to improve, including implementing engaging pedagogies. Empirical studies of service-learning demonstrate significant increases in many indicators of engagement measured by NSSE (Eyler, Giles, Stenson, & Gray, 2001; Kuh, 2008). However, studies that emphasize the influence of service-learning on student engagement in a New Zealand context are uncommon.

As an integral component to the student engagement equation, service-learning has been identified as a pedagogy that increases student engagement in higher education settings (Kuh, 2008). This increase in engagement has been attributed to many different aspects of service-learning (e.g., community-needed service, active/collaborative learning, in/out-of-class learning, self-reflection, and personal growth).

In New Zealand the characteristics Zepke, Leach, and Butler (2009) identified as ways for teachers to augment student engagement—building relationships, prompt feedback, enthusiasm for their subjects, challenging students, and providing opportunities for students to apply knowledge to practical problems—are key characteristics and conditions of service-learning.

ACTUALIZING STUDENTS' EXPERIENCES

With this research base and theoretical context, a Naturalistic Inquiry (Lincoln & Guba, 1985) into the UNIV300 course and student experience with service-learning was implemented. Observation of in/out-of-class experiences and interviews with participants provided the thick description necessary to deepen understanding of the complex relationship between service-learning and student engagement. Furthermore, understanding of these *mold-breaking* experiences provided insight into how the lessons learned from this relationship can be transferred to other education environments.

On the first day of class, Trevor and David welcomed students to what they described as, "the best undergraduate class in the department." They proceeded by informing the students that a method of teaching and learning referred to as "service-learning" would facilitate the course. The students worked in groups of 4–5 on community identified research topics. The instructors handed out the course syllabus, addressed the advantages and disadvantages of service-learning, introduced service-learning research topics to the students, and with this overview attempted to manage the expectations of their students.

This was positive because many of the students had never participated in a service-learning environment before. "I recall a buzz developing throughout the classroom; the students were turning and looking at each other with looks of excitement and nervousness" (Perry, 2009). This first class session, with its initial description of service-learning and justification of chosen pedagogy, represented a purposive effort at developing an environment where the student–teacher relationship may be more interactive, egalitarian, and less hierarchal. Furthermore, similar to cooperation among students and active-learning environments, the communication of expectations is a good practice for undergraduate education (Chickering & Gamson, 1987; Zepke et al., 2009). The first class period set the tone for the rest of the semester.

Practically, these students participated in the following activities and assignments, which served as the scaffolding for their service-learning experiences:

- attended Workshop Weekend;
- prepared critical assessment of research topic;
- offered mid-semester presentation on progress;
- offered final presentation at public class conference;
- prepared written group report;
- prepared individual critique of project research/learning;
- prepared item for community partners;
- participated in final reflection session;
- attended meetings with community partners;
- attended meetings with student group/tutor.

These student activities and assignments represented the many opportunities and conditions attributed to the service-learning environment.

SHINGLES FOR THE ROOF: CATEGORIZED AND UNITIZED DATA FROM THE FIELD

From one of the first observations (May, 2009) to one of the last (November, 2009), the continuity of the types of interactions that occurred and relationships that developed among teachers and students in this course were consistent. Service-learning fundamentally shifts the context of the classroom and concomitantly changes the experiences of students. It seems from within this new context, novel opportunities for students emerge and subsequently influence their engagement (Perry, field notes, 2009). This shift in context is demonstrated by Tabitha:

> It is like we have been put in a test-tube with all this muddy water. The mud, stones, and sands, everything, and we do not know what we are doing because the thing keeps stirring. The more we stir, the less you can see and you get more confused. As the progress continues it stirs faster and faster and eventually the sands and sediments fall to the bottom and you can see through it.

Tabitha went on to describe her group and their engagement with their research topic as the source of energy that stirred her metaphoric centrifuge faster, subsequently clearing her test tube's muddy waters. As the learning environment was influenced by service-learning, the students embraced different opportunities.

A core outcome of these different experiences was a feeling of departing from one's comfort zone by being challenged which was equated to personal growth and development (Eyler et al., 2001). These opportunities were identified in the emergent themes that were triangulated and reconstructed from the students' spoken/written words and observations.

As service-learning shifted the context of what it means to be a student in a classroom, these themes symbolize the different experiences identified and demonstrate ways educators can best engage both eager and reluctant learners (see Figure 19.1):

- different experiences providing opportunities for growth;
- consistently being a part of something internal/external to university;
- active learning through experiencing and thinking for yourself;
- worthwhile intrinsic—due to helping community organizations.

The theme, *being a part of something*, is clarified by Mark as he contextualizes his perspective as a student: "[This class] is taking a step in, like we're a part of something, and we're dealing with real people in the real-world and I think a lot of people are liking that." Mark is alluding to the tacit feeling of

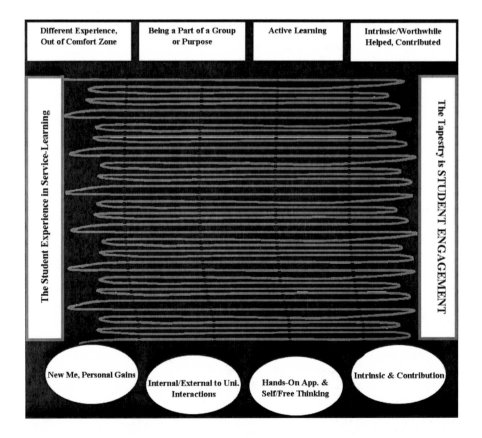

Figure 19.1. A Tapestry of Student Engagement: Created by an Interweaving of Service-Learning Themes Identified from the Student Experience

being a part of something. He uses active description like "taking a step in" and speaks from a communal perspective with the phrase, "*we* are dealing with real people." The "we" he is speaking of is his group and the "real people" and "real world" he is addressing are those community groups external to university (Eyler et al., 2001; Eyler & Giles, 1994).

The *active-learning* theme, based on the students' experiences and subsequent service-learning relationships and influences, represents the opportunity to learn from doing (*ma te mahi e ako ai*), experiencing, and applying what students were learning not only from service-learning experiences, but from total life experiences. In this capacity, active learning seems to be a way we can empower our students to become independent learners as they learn to *think critically*. Megan demonstrated the difference between other classes and her service-learning class in context of active learning.

> I have been involved in many projects with small groups before, but the methods and approaches were often laid out for us. By being introduced to this approach, I have learnt to think critically and attempt to solve a problem that is not 'scenario-based,' but actually beneficial to others outside of university. (Critique, 2009)

Furthermore, this type of environment, which is teeming with high expectations of the students, seems to be one of the sources for engagement (Zepke et al., 2009). Taking the students' internal and external interactions with the university and community groups one step further leads the students to a type of interaction and learning that is actively engaging. The students tend to take ownership in their projects and, subsequently, value their investment of time, resources, and effort.

The final emergent theme is based on the *worthwhile and intrinsic value* students felt from completing the course (Dewey, 1933). Interestingly, the students did not refer to what they were doing for their respective community groups as volunteer service. Although, they did feel it was valuable for the community. This serves as an example of how instructors can enhance students' intrinsic motivation to become successful learners. They can make learning meaningful by using it as a tool for helping the local community.

Mark and Amy, respectively, articulated this perspective clearly with the following points:

> The service-learning process as a whole was great, but for me… the fact it was service-based was really the best aspect. This would have been the first time, for some, where work they do actually contributes to peoples' lives in a real sense.
> The research undertaken helped solve a problem inside a community that are appreciative of what we have offered. This created a sense of pride and fulfillment.

It seems that this particular theme truly separated service-learning from other pedagogies. While interactions with peers and staff in a self-driven, free-thinking environment are pivotal factors in students' experience and engagement, the understanding and perception that their projects were desired by established, local community organizations is a vital factor for students' experiences. This, in turn, created a sense of pride and ownership in the project.

CONCLUSION: OPENING THE NEW HOME

These emergent themes, which are rooted in the thick descriptions of student experience, serve as examples as to how instructors can use engaging pedagogies such as service-learning to *break the mold* of traditional classroom management approaches at the tertiary level. As an offspring of service-learning, these practices and conditions can influence the student experience in order to generate a paradigm shift in students' perspective of what it means to be a student. Service-learning has been shown to be an influential pedagogy for involving, engaging, and motivating students to invest their time, effort, and energy into worthwhile projects. In turn, this makes relevant their learning and frames their understanding within a wider context. This context is based on what the students described as the real world.

As the student experience undulates through the emergent themes of service-learning, students' engagement is influenced in a positive way. Considering that the effects of service-learning on engagement are relatively unresearched in New Zealand higher education, these implications provide insight into practical uses of service-learning for New Zealand and international environments. Ultimately, the power of pedagogy, and particularly that of service-learning, should not go untapped.

NOTE

Pseudonyms are used to maintain anonymity.

REFERENCES

Australian Council for Educational Research (ACER). (2008). *Attracting, engaging and retaining: New conversations about learning.* Victoria, Australia: Author.

Chickering, A., & Gamson, Z (Eds.) (1987). Seven principles for good practice in undergraduate education. *AAHE Bulletin, 39*, 3–7.

Dewey, J. (1933/1986). How we think: A restatement of the relation of reflective thinking to the educative process. In J. Boydston (Ed.), *John Dewey: The later works, 1925-1953,* Volume 8: 1933 (pp. 105–352). Carbondale, IL: Southern Illinois University Press.

Eyler, J., Giles, D., Stenson, C., & Gray, C. (2001). *At a glance: What we know about the effects of service-learning on college students, faculty, institutions and communities, 1993-*

2000 (3rd ed.). Washington, DC: Corporation for Service—Learn and Serve America National Service Learning Clearinghouse.

Giles, D., & Eyler, J. (1994). The theoretical roots of service-learning in John Dewey: Toward a theory of service-learning. *Michigan Journal of Community Service Learning, 1*(1), 77–85.

Kuh, G. (2008). *High-impact educational practices: What they are, who has access to them, and why they matter.* Washington, DC: AAC&U.

Kuh, G. (2009, July). *High-impact activities and implications for curriculum design.* Paper presented at Queensland University, Australia.

Kuh, G., Kinzie, J., Buckley, J., Bridges, B., & Hayek, J. (2007). *Piecing together the student success puzzle: Research, propositions, and recommendations.* ASHE Higher Education Report, *32*(5). San Francisco, CA: Jossey-Bass.

Kuh, G., Kinzie, J., Schuh, J., & Whitt, E. (2005). *Student success in college: Creating conditions that matter.* San Francisco, CA: Jossey-Bass.

Lincoln, Y., & Guba E. (1985). *Naturalistic inquiry.* Beverly Hills, CA: Sage.

Nelson Laird, T., Chen, D., & Kuh, G. (2008). Classroom practices in institutions with higher-than-expected persistence rates: What student engagement data tell us. *New Directions for Teaching and Learning, 115*, 85–99.

Parker, E., Myers, N., Higgins, C., Oddsson T., Price, M., & Gould, T. (2009). More than experiential learning or volunteering: A case study of community service-learning within the Australian context. *Higher Education Research & Development, 28*, 585–596.

Perry, L. (2011). *A naturalistic inquiry of service-learning in New Zealand university classrooms: Determining and illuminating the impact on student engagement.* Unpublished Dissertation. University of Canterbury, New Zealand.

Zepke, N., Leach, L., & Butler, P. (2009). The role of teacher-student interactions in tertiary student engagement. *New Zealand Journal of Education Studies, 44*(1), 69–82.

Chapter Twenty

"I teach like you are all gifted": Leading Lowest Track Students to Become Confident Mathematics Learners

Della R. Leavitt and Erin N. Washington

I will never tear a child down; I will build them up. When they see my eyes well up with tears, they realize that I mean it: "You can do it." It is not necessarily a spiritual philosophy; it should be an educational philosophy. If you don't have that, you should not be allowed to teach. (Ms. Henry in Leavitt, 2010, p. 58)

"DON'T BELIEVE ANYONE WHO SAYS YOU WILL NOT AMOUNT TO ANYTHING!"

Ms. Henry, one of two African American teachers at Neely School, had been away for two days on funeral leave for her cousin, who was shot and killed senselessly. Upon her return to her lowest track seventh-grade mathematics class, she began by asking students, "What happened while I was gone?"

Parker is an African American male student who rides to this White, working-class neighborhood magnet school on what he once pointed out as the "Africa bus." He is not afraid to speak his mind, and quickly replied:

"We were working on the problems you left us and helping each other like we always do. The substitute told us not to talk. I told her this is how we work. Then she told us 'we would never amount to anything.'"

Parker recalled the exchange angrily. "I told her what did she know, she was just an old substitute."

Ms. Henry looked around the room at this lowest track class of 11 students. There were six males (three African American, two White, and one Chinese American) and five females (three White, one African American, and one Latina). She paused and said fervently:

> I heard about this, but I wanted to hear it from you. I believe in each of you and what you can do. No one should *ever* tell you that you will not amount to anything. Don't believe it. But know that when it comes to fighting an adult who has power, be careful. Students will rarely win a battle like this. (Leavitt, 2010, pp. 57–58)

MS. HENRY'S TEACHING PHILOSOPHY AND GOALS FOR STUDENTS

Ms. Henry focuses on what it means to serve as an excellent teacher for those who others believe cannot excel. She recognizes how at Neely, a school set in a neighborhood notorious for racial hostilities, "I wasn't allowed to teach the gifted track." She recalls, "I told my [lowest tracked] students: 'I teach you like you are all gifted.'" And she did. Ms. Henry had confidence in her students, both in what they could learn in mathematics class and who they could be.

> My whole goal as a teacher is to make them better than me. All their creative talents and insights and experiences will allow them to do something wonderful some day. If you empower children and believe in them, they will know that we are here for a greater goal. [They believe] "I can do this. I can do more." (Leavitt, 2010, p. 115)

Ms. Henry's practices are exemplified by Mary McLeod Bethune's teaching tenets to teach with "head-hands-heart" and with the motto "enter to learn, depart to serve" (Hanson, 2003). These watchwords connect to Ms. Henry's dedication to underserved students and to the teaching profession. She is a teacher with deep mathematics content knowledge; however, as Martin (2007) posited, a teacher's content knowledge mastery is necessary but not sufficient to teach students who are not expected to achieve. In her practice, Ms. Henry is an example of the *culturally relevant teacher* who supports her students' (a) mathematics achievement gains, (b) cultural identities inside and outside of the classroom, and (c) development of critical sociopolitical perspectives (Ladson-Billings, 1995).

EXEMPLARY TEACHERS COUNTER STEREOTYPES ABOUT WHO CAN *DO MATH*

Teachers of students who are in danger of being denied opportunities to learn mathematics, science, and engineering must counter conflicting societal, educational, and internalized messages about who can and cannot *do math*. Martin (2009) stated that society has developed a racial hierarchy of mathematics ability that places White and Asian students at the top, and African American, Latinos/as, and Native Americans at the bottom. In many schools, student tracking reinforces societal norms about who can achieve in mathematics related fields (McGee, 2009; Oakes, 1985; Tate & Rousseau, 2002).

Ms. Henry reverses these expectations for her lowest track students. She is a proud African American woman with firm convictions about her purpose. Her teaching identity takes on "the form of tales of service and servant, of doing one's public duty and obeying, or not, orders from above" (Connelly & Clandinin, 1999, p. 172). Such teachers' identities are "stories to live by" and reveal how teachers' stories fit together forming a "theoretical puzzle to link knowledge, context, and identity" (Connelly & Clandinin, p. 4). Ms. Henry's practice describes how "teachers must know their students, reach out to them with care and understanding in order to create a bridge from the known to the not-yet-known" (Ayers, 2004, p. 25).

INSIDE MS. HENRY'S SEVENTH-GRADE MATHEMATICS CLASSROOM

Introduction to Ms. Henry and her Students

Ms. Henry is in her thirties. She earned an undergraduate degree in engineering and an MBA. She is a deeply spiritual woman who followed what she declared a calling to teach mathematics in the same large urban public-school district where she lives and attended school. She formally entered the classroom through a university-sponsored alternative certification program. Fulfilling rigorous criteria, she became a National Board Certified Teacher after completing the minimum four years of teaching experience. These descriptions from her 7th grade mathematics class are culled from videotaped classroom observations and interview excerpts that took place during the year she compiled her successful portfolio for National Board Certification.

The lesson excerpt takes place mid-way through the year. Nine of the eleven seventh-grade students are present. Ms. Henry planned a whole-class discussion, and arranged the students' desks in a square U-shape before the students entered. Giving the students autonomy is atypical within this school; here students freely select their own seats.

Often the females choose one side of the "U" and the males sit together facing them on the opposite side. Two male students are absent on this day. One is Mychal, an African American male, who often misses class. He must take three city buses to get to Neely School which is located far from his neighborhood. The other missing student is Stan. Stan is a White male student with special needs. Sometimes Stan is in school, but not in Ms. Henry's mathematics class because he is receiving other services. However, Stan is often a valuable contributor in her class.

This lowest track class has an unusually small number of students to accommodate an unplanned hiring of a teacher after the school year began. This action forced redistribution of the students among three full-time middle-grades mathematics teachers. Ms. Henry's students have formed a cohesive classroom discourse community often found in more privileged school settings (Boaler, 2002). They follow recognized standards where students openly ask questions, make conjectures, and respectfully challenge fellow students and the teacher (National Council of Teachers of Mathematics, 2000).

Students are respectful to each other. Ms. Henry also demonstrates respect with the classroom norm allowing students to speak up freely and talk to each other without needing to be recognized with hands raised. Also, unlike other classes, Ms. Henry explicitly permits students to leave the room at will to take care of personal needs.

Today's Lesson: Addition of Positive and Negative Integers

Ms. Henry begins the lesson by testing students' prior knowledge. She asks: "True or false? The sum of two negatives integers is always negative." Sally is the first student to speak up. "False, because a negative plus a negative is positive." Ms. Henry asks her to support her statement with an example. Sally replies, "Negative five plus negative five is ten." Ms. Henry asks if all agree, and the students begin to talk among themselves. Parker ventures, "Sally is half-way correct, because it will equal zero." Ms. Henry follows the students' openly spoken confusion and writes three contradictory number sentences on the board. She asks students to choose which of the following is true and to explain the reasoning for their choice:

(1) $(-5) + (-5)$ $= (+10)$

(2) $(-5) + (-5)$ $= 0$

(3) $(-5) + (-5)$ $= (-10)$

Alicia uses her hands to accompany her verbal exploration. She says that adding a positive number takes you "this way" while adding a negative number takes you back "that way" tracing an imaginary line in front of her;

first pointing in one direction and then in reverse. Ms. Henry summarizes Alicia's contributions and introduces the mathematical concept of opposites: "When you add a number plus its opposite you get zero. With negative five plus negative five you do not get zero." This reasoning eliminates number sentence (2), because they conclude you must add opposite numbers for the sum to equal zero. Ms. Henry brings students together to agree that Statement (2) cannot be true.

Your brain is the greatest calculator there is. Ms. Henry now asks students to consider only the first and third number sentences. "Which one is true or which one is false?" she queries. The students begin to work quietly on their own; some use calculators. As she circulates, Ms. Henry cautions students not to rely on the calculators without first thinking about whether or not the answer makes sense: "If you put it in the calculator, you will have to tell me why it's true. Your brain is the greatest calculator there is, so whatever comes up on that screen, you have to tell me why that is." She pushes students to recall the relationship between multiplication and addition. Ms. Henry also urges students to have confidence in their ideas.

Diana recites the general rules for multiplication of signed integers from yesterday's lesson. She reasons that $(-5) + (-5)$ is the same as (-5) times (2) and the product must be a negative 10. Her answer supports the conclusion that the third number sentence must be true. She counters Sally's initial conjecture that a negative plus a negative is a positive number. In these exchanges, Ms. Henry patiently demonstrates high expectations for students' mathematical arguments demanding support for their reasoning.

Ms. Henry is explicitly aware of her approach to teach mathematics toward students' conceptual understanding.

> I always ask them questions, "so how do you know?" And it comes out in their speaking. "I tried this, because…" They always justify whatever they did, and it is so empowering for them. And it is a wonderful thing for me to hear, because it shows me that they are learning. (Ms. Henry in Leavitt, 2010, p. 90)

Duayne surprises classmates with mathematical justification

Duayne often appears as if he is not paying attention. Now he is looking away. After Diana's explanation, Ms. Henry asks Duayne: "Duayne, did you hear what Diana was saying? Do you agree with her?" Duayne answers crisply with a reprise of Diana's answer. He may have been looking away, yet he repeats Diana's answer in detail. He adds how he was thinking along that line of reasoning, too, explaining he was checking the rules he had written into his notebook.

Ms. Henry displays approval, adding her endorsement of "good support" for Duayne's explanation. Here Ms. Henry shows off Duayne's acumen to the whole class. She lifts him up as one who can *do math*. This is also an example of how she values how students learn from each other:

> If I have another student who synthesizes what I've taught and they say it in a
> different way that is more accessible to all of my levels of students, I know
> that everyone learns. Sometimes the way I word things, all of my students
> don't pick up on what I'm trying to say. (Ms. Henry, personal communication)

MS. HENRY'S ADVOCACY FOR STUDENTS GOES BEYOND MATHEMATICS TEACHING

Ms. Henry is dedicated in her role as teacher to serve as students' mathematics guide. She also offered support to several students in and out of school and beyond the mathematics. At times, she opposed the majority of her teacher colleagues in order to stand up when she perceived an injustice toward a student. Parker was one student Ms. Henry mentored in order for him to learn to negotiate the "culture of power" (Delpit, 1988) he had to face at Neely School. Ms. Henry describes Parker as "having a way with words" and standing up for himself. "Other teachers thought he could be a trouble maker. But he wasn't. He was just a really bright kid, a smart kid, a natural leader" (Leavitt, 2010, p.144). Parker now considers himself someone who recognizes the value of learning mathematics.

Parker Stays in Place as First African American Student Council President

In a close race, Parker was elected the first African American student council president at the school. The Neely upper grade teachers tried to remove him from his position for what Ms. Henry considered a minor out-of-school incident. Ms. Henry stepped in. She remembered thinking, "I didn't care what they thought of me. You are not putting him off of student council. He wasn't even in there good" (Leavitt, 2010, p. 144). Two years later, Parker's academic progress qualified him to advance to the citywide high school science fair competition.

Tanya Gains Confidence: She Trusts Because Ms. Henry Cares

Tanya is the only African American female student in this class. She describes herself as a shy person who likes mathematics. She acknowledges that she often has good ideas in class, but admits that she rarely raises her hand. Tanya relates that Ms. Henry has privately urged her to increase her visibility to "say that out loud, so people know you know what you are talking about" (Leavitt, 2010, p. 116). When Ms. Henry calls Tanya to the board, she does not hesitate, although she would rarely volunteer to stand up to share her ideas.

Tanya describes Ms. Henry as a caring teacher similar to her own mother, who encourages her: "If this is where your mind is at, then you should be able to do it." Tanya remembers that "one day when [Ms. Henry] was absent, the [substitute] teacher told us 'You won't amount to anything.'" Tanya speaks with emotion recalling Ms. Henry's words to the class. She remembers Ms. Henry's watchwords: "the next time people tell you that, you say, 'I *am* going to amount to something.'" Tanya adds, "She really cares about [our] education" (Leavitt, 2010, p. 116-117).

THE MEASURE OF TEACHERS WHO GO BEYOND MATHEMATICS

As a mathematics teacher, a mentor, and a student advocate, Ms. Henry gives all she can to empower her students. How she enacts those roles has potentially life-changing impact for many transitional middle-grade students, particularly for students who are not expected to achieve mathematics mastery. Ms. Henry's demonstrated content knowledge frees her to explore paths for her students to find ways to believe in themselves as mathematics learners and take on life and societal challenges. Yet schools and districts are increasingly diminishing teachers' worth by ranking their value based on students' standardized test scores. Uplifting examples of Ms. Henry and so many dedicated teachers who share similar values of integrity and student empowerment are truly beyond measures.

NOTE

All names are pseudonyms.

REFERENCES

Ayers, W. C. (2004). *Teaching the personal and the political: Essays on hope and justice.* New York, NY: Teachers College Press.

Boaler, J. (2002). *Experiencing school mathematics: Traditional and reform approaches to teaching and their impact on student learning.* Mahwah, NJ: Lawrence Erlbaum.

Connelly, F. M., & Clandinin, D. J. (1999). *Shaping a professional identity: Stories of educational practice.* New York, NY: Teachers College Press.

Delpit, L. (1988). The silenced dialogue: Power and pedagogy in educating other people's children. *Harvard Educational Review, 58,* 280–297.

Hanson, J. A. (2003). *Mary McLeod Bethune and Black women's political activism.* Columbia, MO: University of Missouri Press.

Ladson-Billings, G. (1995). Toward a theory of culturally relevant pedagogy. *American Educational Research Journal, 32,* 465–491.

Leavitt, D. R. (2010). *"Meek, but not weak!:" A resilient Black female mathematics teacher composes a purposeful life* (Unpublished doctoral dissertation). Chicago, IL: University of Illinois at Chicago.

Martin, D. B. (2007). Beyond missionaries or cannibals: Who should teach mathematics to African American Children? *High School Journal, 91*(1), 6–28.

Martin, D. B. (2009). Researching race in mathematics education, *Teachers College Record, 111*(2), 295-338.

McGee, E. O. (2009). *Chronicles of success: Black college students negotiating success in mathematics and engineering.* Unpublished doctoral dissertation. Chicago, IL: University of Illinois at Chicago.

National Council of Teachers of Mathematics (NCTM). (2000). *Principles and standards for school mathematics.* Reston, VA: Author.

Oakes, J. (1985). *Keeping track: How schools structure inequality.* New Haven, CT: Yale University Press.

Tate, W., & Rousseau, C. (2002). Access and opportunity: The political and social context in mathematics education. In L. English (Ed.), *Handbook of international research in mathematics education* (pp. 271–300). Mahwah, NJ: Lawrence Erlbaum.

Afterword: Fostering Engagement, Motivation, and Empowerment: Why?

Laura J. Shea Doolan

Imagine teacherless discussions. *Believe it*! Imagine students conducting investigative reporting and research during recess, with no complaints about whose turn it is on the swing. *Why?* Because, how refreshing would it be that children and adolescents, throughout their mandatory formative, schooling years, engage in true dialogue with each other in authentic, real world settings, at their schools! Furthermore, research studies on the relationship between teaching strategies that foster student engagement, motivation, and empowerment (SEME) reveal a dramatic influence on positive student learning—academically and socially—that might also support the development of life-long learning communities.

These concepts resonate in this volume entitled *Breaking the Mold of Education: Innovative and Successful Practices for Student Engagement, Empowerment, and Motivation for the 21st Century*. All contributors to this edited volume—with ideas on encouraging teachers to better assist individuals' learning—detail how to employ numerous strategies as well as focus on the importance of learners' academic achievement. Their innovative work underscores how SEME may facilitate diverse pupils' ownership of, and investment into, their learning.

The ideas presented in this book *transcend* learners mastering a specific objective and *transform* students learning academic content into individuals who should become life-long, motivated learners and engaged, positive contributors to humankind. For example, as revealed by one practitioner, the "slippery slope of boredom" of mastering an objective was eradicated because students were taught collegially and were provided with *choice* and *control* over their own learning environment, a learning-style element iden-

179

tified more than 30 years ago by pioneering researchers Rita and Kenneth Dunn (Dunn, White, & Zenhausern, 1982; Shea Doolan, 2004). Consequently, when students are invited to take ownership, thoughtful dialogue ensued and a respectful, strong, learning community was established. Therefore, these students are possible potential, global, contributing citizens.

Furthermore, *Breaking the Mold's* contributors identified common core components in which teachers and students should be engaged, to reduce lackadaisical demeanors in the classroom. (In the future that could be transposed to employees' and employers' actions during company meetings.) Another educator detailed an example of student empowerment and how it was fostered by having a student self-regulate her participation in her own learning, which then led to self-monitoring of her perseverance, and adaptive skills, all essential aspects to optimal academic and social success, especially when transitioning from one grade (or employment) level to another.

Breaking the Mold's researchers and practitioners support the ideas that past and current educators realize(d) what must constitute a progressive, inclusive society to better mankind. This is exemplified by Plato, who stated, "Do not train youths to learning by force and harshness, but direct them to it by what amuses [engages] their minds so that you may be able to discover with accuracy the peculiar bent of the genius of each" (as cited in Wandberg & Rohwer, 2003, p. 127) and believed that teaching to the uniqueness of each learner would best benefit society. Confucius also emphasized the concept that teachers were leaders and instrumental in promoting social change and justice, but to do so they needed to attend to the nuances of their students' learning characteristics (Ornstein & Levine, 2006).

Hence, whether learners evidence SEME due to literacy and language strategies, music, movement, the arts, reflective practices or a combination of all—as professed in *Breaking the Mold*—when they are engaged, motivated, and empowered, the culture of their schools and the communities and partnerships, served by these schools' stakeholders, should evidence a positive heritage, thus, promoting social justice and social harmony, and, hopefully, in as benevolent a manner as Confucius would expect.

Furthermore, during this time, if education stakeholders believe nationally and internationally complex solutions to today's and the future's global problems are a priority, they need to collaborate and unmold certain myths about teaching techniques to better assess the unique configuration of how today's youth can best learn, critically think, and endeavor to find resolutions to the world's tribulations.

Break the mold! What does that really mean? How is it really accomplished?

1. Yes, educators need to prepare students to learn on their own.
2. Yes, educators need to personalize aspects of the learning process.

3. Yes, teachers need to be careful not to overreact and hyper-individual-ize curriculum (Willingham & Daniel, 2012).
4. Yes, "every student needs 'peacock' moments of success so class-mates accept them as intellectual contributors" (Tomlinson & Javius, 2012, p. 33).
5. Yes, standards are needed.
6. Yes, educators need to personalize aspects of the learning process, through engagement, motivation, and empowerment, so students can best learn and meticulously meet the standards.
7. Yes, teach everyone so they can "gift" back to mankind and shatter the mold, and create new prototypes, when needed!

Breaking the Mold shares strategies that can be used to enhance student accomplishment. Its editors Audrey Cohan and Andrea Honigsfeld have as-sembled practitioners and researchers who demonstrate how it *is* accom-plished.

REFERENCES

Dunn, R., White, R. M., & Zenhausern, R. (1982). An investigation of responsible versus less responsible students. *Illinois School Research and Development Journal, 19*(1), 19–24.

Ornstein, A., & Levine, D. (2006). *Foundations of education* (9th ed.). Boston, MA: Houghton Mifflin.

Shea Doolan, L. J. (2004). *A historical analysis of the international learning styles network and its impact on instructional innovation.* Lampeter, UK: The Edwin Mellen Press.

Tomlinson, C. A., & Javius, E. L. (2012). Teach up for excellence. *Educational Leadership, 69*(5), 28–33.

Wandberg, R., & Rohwer, J. (2003). *Teaching to the standards of effective practice: A guide to becoming a successful teacher.* Boston, MA: Allyn & Bacon.

Willingham, D., & Daniel, D. (2012). Teaching to what students have in common. *Educational Leadership, 69*(5), 16–21.

Contributors

Rebecca Ambrose, PhD, is an associate professor of mathematics education, University of California, Davis. Dr. Ambrose collaborates with teachers to better understand children's mathematical thinking, especially the thinking of English language learners. She is also actively engaged in research training and teaches research seminars for new teachers as part of their MA program. The inquiry work described in her chapter came from one of the projects from the seminar.

Eve Bernstein, EdD, is an assistant professor in the Department of Family Nutrition and Exercise Science at Queens College, City University of New York. She has had extensive experience teaching physical education and martial arts. She has focused her work on the structure and implementation of competitive activities in middle school physical education classes.

Patricia M. Breslin, MEd, has been teaching middle school English at Bridgeway Island K–8 School in West Sacramento, California for four years. She earned her master's degree in education at the University of California, Davis. She continues to lecture to undergraduate education classes on effective, student-centered teaching methods. Her interests include promoting equity in education as well as finding innovative instructional methods that encourage students to take ownership of their learning.

Peter Cammock, PhD, is director of the Masters of Business Administration program at the University of Canterbury, New Zealand. He is the author of two leadership books, *The Dance of Leadership* (Prentice Hall, 2001, 2003) and *The Spirit of Leadership* (Leadership Press, 2008). Dr. Cammock has over 25 years of experience in teaching under/postgraduate students and has a strong interest in researching and applying innovative teaching methods.

Vinesh Chandra, ScEdD, is a senior lecturer in education at the Queensland University of Technology, Australia. His teaching areas are ICT and Technology. His research interests include the investigation of technology-rich learning environments and their impact on students' perceptions and their learning outcomes.

Andrew P. Charland, MEd, is currently a fourth/fifth-grade multiage teacher at A.B. Combs Leadership Magnet Elementary School in Raleigh, North Carolina. He received his BA from Western Michigan University and MEd from Marygrove College, Michigan. He has 10 years of elementary teaching experience.

Evelyn M. Connolly, EdD, received her doctorate in literacy studies from Hofstra University, New York, in 2008. Her interest and research in multiliteracies and multimodal learning inform her pedagogy. She has integrated visual art, drama, and technology in her college and public school classrooms and workshops for over 20 years. Her recent book, *The Incorporation of Multimedia and Multimodal Learning Tools: A Case Study of Digital Storytelling in a High School English Class* was published by The Edwin Mellen Press in 2011.

Sara Cortés-Gómez, PhD, is an assistant professor of developmental communication and education at the University of Alcalá, Spain. Dr. Cortés holds a degree in psycho-pedagogy and recently finished her doctoral thesis, *Imaginary Worlds, Virtual Reality: Video Games in the Classroom* (2010). Her main research focus is on analyzing and fostering the creation of new educational spaces where new technologies become literacy practices.

Joanne Kilgour Dowdy, PhD, is a professor at Kent State University, Ohio. A theatre graduate of the Juilliard School, Dr. Dowdy uses her drama training to prepare teachers for the literacy classroom. Her major research interests include documenting the experiences of Black women involved in education from adult basic literacy to higher education, and she has written and edited seven books with her training and those interests in mind, including *GED Stories: Black Women & Their Struggle for Social Equity* (Peter Lang, 2003), *Ph.D. Stories: Conversations with My Sisters* (Hampton Press, 2009), and *Teaching Drama in the Classroom: A Toolbox for Teachers* (Sense Publishers, 2011).

Beverly S. Faircloth, PhD, is an associate professor in the Department of Teacher Education and Higher Education at the University of North Carolina at Greensboro. Her research interests include adolescent sense of school belonging and identity development, as well as other motivational processes that support school engagement. She earned her doctorate at the University of North Carolina at Chapel Hill.

Robin E. Finnan-Jones, EdD, is the New York City Department of Education CFN 410 Deputy Network Leader for School Improvement. She has been an adjunct professor at St. John's University in the TESOL department, and at Long Island University in the field of reading. Dr. Finnan-Jones is a former New York City Department of Education District 24 Queens administrator and teacher.

Sioux Finney, MA, uses the arts to teach seventh and eighth grade social studies to future civic leaders at Woodford County Middle School in Versailles, Kentucky. Earlier careers include youth ministry in the Presbyterian Church and entertainment director for Silver Dollar City, Inc. Middle school is her favorite place to be, as every day is a new adventure.

María Ruth García-Pernía is an assistant professor of developmental communication and education at the University of Alcalá, Spain. She works as a researcher and is a member of the research group: Grupo Imágenes Palabras e Ideas (Images, Words, and Ideas Group: http://uah-gipi.org/ingles.htm). In 2007, she started collaborating with the group and, at present, she is writing her doctoral thesis. She is interested in learning environments and analyzing the role of the new technologies as well as how they transform the reality around us.

Anne Gibbone, EdD, is an assistant professor in the Exercise Science, Health Studies, Physical Education and Sport Management Department at Adelphi University, New York. Over the past 10 years, her teaching has included teacher preparation, middle school physical education and adapted physical education in addition to coaching a variety of sports. She has focused much of her work on physical education and educational technology implementation for health, fitness, and physical activity.

Peter Hoffman-Kipp, PhD, is Transition Point and Major Assessment Coordinator for the Richard W. Riley College of Education at Walden University, Minnesota, where he received the 2010 President's Award for Faculty Excellence. His research interests include teacher learning and reflection, especially around issues of teacher identity, diversity, and the politics of education.

Pilar Lacasa, PhD, is professor of developmental communication and education at the University of Alcalá, Spain. Dr. Lacasa leads the research group: Grupo Imágenes Palabras e Ideas (Images, Words, and Ideas Group: http://uah-gipi.org/ingles.htm). The group has developed innovative methodological approaches in a number of areas and has led the debate about the development of teacher training programs and educational policy in Spain. Dr. Lacasa has been a visiting scholar at the University of Utah, the University of British Columbia, and at Massachusetts Institute of Technology.

Kate Larken, MA, is a publisher, musician, educator, playwright, journalist, producer, and entrepreneur. She is the author of *Arts & Humanities: A Student Handbook* (middle school edition) and its supplemental *Teacher Resource Book* (EvaMedia, 2006) as well as *Teddy's Piece* (MotesBooks, 2011). She is currently working on a novel, *S LAN T*. She was a fellow in the Appalachian Sound Archives at Berea College (2011), was awarded the Sallie Bingham Prize (Kentucky Foundation for Women, 2010), and has recorded several collections of original songs (Nekked-Rekkedz, 1995–2010).

Wendy J. LaRue, PhD, is Head of School and co-founder of Odyssey Montessori and owner of AhHa! Consulting, LLC, which provides research consultation, academic editing, professional development training, and parent education programs. Her research interests include nontraditional education, school reform, experiential education, child development, parent involvement, peaceful approaches to parenting, and provision of children's services.

Della R. Leavitt, PhD, recently completed a postdoctoral position as a Research Associate with an NSF-sponsored Math/Science Partnership at Rutgers University. She is now a Research Consultant in Program Evaluation for arts-intergrated projects in the Chicago Public Schools. She continues to work toward the empowerment of teachers in order to equitably advance students' opportunities to learn challenging mathematics. Dr. Leavitt earned her PhD in 2010 from the University of Illinois at Chicago's College of Education.

Amanda Levido, MLI, is a media arts researcher at Queensland University of Technology, Australia. She currently works with teachers to implement media arts into their classroom curriculum. Her research interests consider the work young people do in informal learning spaces.

Ulana Lysniak, EdD, is an adjunct assistant professor in the Department of Physical Education and Exercise Science at Brooklyn College, City University of New York. She has taught physical education pedagogy classes, on both the graduate and undergraduate level, for 20 years. Her research focus has been on teaching strategies for low motor-skilled students. She also teaches fitness and conditioning.

Rut Martínez-Borda is a professor of developmental communication and education at the University of Alcalá, Spain. Dr. Martínez-Borda works on videogames, new technologies, and new literacies. Her current research on the topic of computer games and narratives is supported by the Ministry of Culture and Education. She has been a visiting scholar at the Institute of Education at the University of London, University of Westminster of London, University of Delaware, and collaborates with other research groups at the Universidad Autónoma de Madrid, Universidad Nacional de Educación a Distancia (UNED), and Universidad de Córdoba, Spain.

Nancye E. McCrary, EdD, is an associate professor of education and instructional designer at St. Catherine College in Kentucky. Her research interests include critical pedagogy and social justice education. Dr. McCrary serves as a member of the Rouge Forum steering committee, consulting editor of *Educational Technology Research & Development*, and a co-principle investigator on the middle level social studies and language arts professional development partnership for the center for collaborative literacy development.

Samuel D. Miller, PhD, is a professor and associate dean for academic and student affairs at the University of North Carolina at Greensboro. His research interests focus on the effects of academic tasks on students' motivation and learning in elementary and middle school classrooms. He received his doctorate from the University of Michigan.

Audrey Figueroa Murphy, EdD, is an assistant professor of TESOL at St. John's University in New York. Prior to joining St. John's, she was a bilingual educator and principal, eventually accepting the position of network leader for 20 schools within the New York City Department of Education. Her research focuses on English language learners and the self-efficacy of teachers and administrators who provide them with instructional support.

Billy O'Steen, PhD, focuses his teaching and research on curriculum design and professional development with a particular emphasis on experiential education and service-learning. In his previous and current positions in education, he has engaged with service-learning as a practitioner and researcher. In addition, in his previous appointment of assistant professor at North Carolina State University, his affiliation with the service-learning program there was noted with two Provost's Certificates of Engagement. He was also named a Service-Learning Fellow.

Shannon T. Page, BA, is currently a fourth/fifth-grade multiage teacher at AB Combs Leadership Magnet Elementary School in Raleigh, North Carolina. She received her BA in liberal arts/elementary education with a minor in special education at Longwood University. She has five years of elementary teaching experience.

Lane Perry, PhD, currently serves as an assistant professor in the College of Education at the University of Canterbury in Christchurch, New Zealand. He has recently been appointed as director of the Center for Service Learning at Western Carolina University in North Carolina. He has published and presented extensively in the field of service-learning, community engagement, and student leadership development, and served as a co-editor for the second volume of *The International Undergraduate Journal for Service-Learning, Leadership, and Social Change.*

Meg Goldner Rabinowitz, MA, MS, is a visiting lecturer at the Graduate School of Education at the University of Pennsylvania, where she teaches secondary education in the Teacher Education Program and the Teach for America Program. She currently teaches high school English and Media Studies at Germantown Friends School, a Quaker independent school in Philadelphia, Pennsylvania. Her work focuses on issues of equity, social justice, and inclusion, and she is keenly interested in incorporating visual arts into the study of language and literature.

Thomas G. Reio, Jr., PhD, is the interim associate dean of graduate studies in the College of Education and associate professor of adult education and human resource development at Florida International University. He is active in his research concerning the links between curiosity, risk-taking and learning across the lifespan. He is currently working on a book about adolescent curiosity and risk-taking where he highlights the positive roles that curiosity and risk-taking play in fostering psychologically healthy development during adolescence.

Heather Rogers Haverback, PhD, is an educational psychologist who is currently a professor of elementary education at Towson University, Maryland. She has taught elementary and middle school in the United States and Japan. Her research interests include teacher efficacy, preservice reading teachers, reading education, and middle-level education.

Angela K. Salmon, EdD, is associate professor and program leader in the early childhood education program at Florida International University. Her interest in the interplay between cognition and language and literacy development has led her to conduct research in areas such as thinking, habits of mind, metacognition, teacher's discourse in the classroom, and the development of communities of practice. She is founder and leader of the Visible Thinking South Florida initiative and is currently working on a book on making thinking visible in young children.

Mara Sapon-Shevin, EdD, is a professor of inclusive education at Syracuse University, New York, where she prepares teachers for heterogeneous, inclusive classrooms. She is the author of *Because We Can Change the World: A Practical Guide to Building Cooperative, Inclusive Classroom Communities* (Corwin Press, 2010) and *Widening the Circle: The Power of Inclusive Classrooms* (Beacon Press, 2007). Dr. Sapon-Shevin's interests include anti-oppressive education, anti-bullying, and using the arts to teach for social justice.

April A. Scott, MEd, is currently a doctoral student and teaching assistant in the College of Education at North Carolina State University. Her focus is literacy education. She received her BA and MEd from the University of North Carolina at Chapel Hill. She has eight years of teaching experience and is currently teaching an online content area reading course for preservice teachers.

Yolanda Sealey-Ruiz, PhD, is an assistant professor of English education at Teachers College, Columbia University, New York. Her research interests include racial literacy in urban teacher education, the literate lives of Black and Latino male high school students, culturally responsive pedagogy, and the educational trajectories of African American female college reentry students.

Laura J. Shea Doolan, EdD, is a professor at Molloy College, Rockville Centre, New York. Dr. Shea Doolan teaches graduate courses in action research, multiculturalism, literacy, foundations of education, and critical issues in early childhood education. She has conducted several studies on learning styles (differentiated instruction), authored the book *A Historical Analysis of the International Learning Styles Network and Its Impact on Instructional Innovation* (The Edwin Mellen Press, 2004), and also has authored articles and chapters on learning styles. She is a board member of the International Learning Styles Network (ILSN), serves as its historian, and is a national and international presenter.

Hiller A. Spires, PhD, is a professor in the College of Education and a senior research fellow at the Friday Institute for Educational Innovation at North Carolina State University. She received her PhD from the University of

South Carolina in literacy education. Dr. Spires's research focuses on the effects of digital literacies on learning, including emerging literacies associated with gaming environments and Web 2.0 applications. She co-directs the New Literacies Collaborative (www.newlit.org).

Mary T. Toepfer, PhD, currently teaches in Ohio at Hiram College in the English and education departments and at Kent State University in the department of teaching, learning, and curriculum studies. Her major research interests include improvisational drama, process writing, literacy strategies across the content areas, and multi-genre research papers. Dr. Toepfer has published several articles and chapters on these subjects, including "Bring the Story to Life: Using Drama with Literature" in *Teaching Drama in the Classroom: A Toolbox for Teachers* (Sense Publishers, 2011).

Erin N. Washington, NBCT, is currently in her tenth year as an Educator in Chicago Public Schools. She worked as a middle grades math teacher, district math specialist, Area math coach, and now serves as an Instructional Support Leader for a Network of over thirty schools on Chicago's South Side. Erin works with Principals and Assistant Principals to help them provide high caliber, rigorous instruction to children in an impoverished community. Erin recently earned her Masters of Education degree in Educational Leadership in 2011.

Kenneth C. Williams, MA, shares his experience and expertise as a recognized trainer, speaker, coach, and consultant in education and leadership. He is the chief visionary officer of Unfold The Soul, a company dedicated to inspiring individuals and teams to perform at the highest level. Skilled in developing productive, student-focused learning environments, Mr. Williams is a distinguished teacher, mentor, public speaker, and school leader. He is a contributing author to *The Collaborative Administrator* (Solution Tree Press, 2009) and the author of *Essentials for Principals: Creating Physical and Emotional Security in Schools* (Solution Tree Press/NAESP, 2012).

Susan N. Wood, PhD, was most recently director of middle school teacher education and the Bluegrass Writing Project at the University of Kentucky. In 2012, she returned to the classroom to teach reading in grades 3–12 at the smallest high school in Florida.

Annette Woods, PhD, is an associate professor within the faculty of education at Queensland University of Technology, Australia. She is co-editor of *Curriculum, Syllabus Design and Equity: A Primer and a Model* (Routledge, 2012), and researches in the fields of social justice, literacies, curriculum and pedagogy, and school reform. She currently leads a four-year funded project which is investigating school reform for improved literacy outcomes in low SES and culturally diverse schools.

Judy W. Yu, EdD, is the Founding Executive Director of Reach®: Research. Educate. Aspire. Change. History.® REACH® is an educational consulting firm based in New York City. The mission of REACH® is to collaborate with children, youth, parents, schools, and community leaders as active participants to conduct research on the challenges of curriculum and instruction in urban schools to educational change. Dr. Yu is also a teaching artist at the Museum of Chinese in America where she is developing the first Asian American studies program for pre-school children in New York City.

David Zyngier, PhD, is a senior lecturer in the faculty of education at Monash University, Australia, and a former school principal and public school teacher. His research focuses on teacher pedagogies that engage all students but in particular, how these can improve academic and social outcomes for children from Cultural, Linguistic and Economincally Disenfranchised (CLED) communities. He is Co-director (with Dr. Paul R. Carr) of the Global Doing Democracy Research Project which in 2013 was awarded major grants from the Canadian and Australian Research Councils. He is on the editorial board of a number of prestigious education journals and a public commentator on education issues in Australia.